They Came Singing:

Songs from California's History

Compiled, edited and arranged by Karen Arlen, Margaret Batt and Nancie Kester
Illustrations by Karen Arlen, Margaret Batt and Nancie Kester
Book design, calligraphy and maps by Nancie Kester
Singable Spanish translations by Margaret Batt
Music layout by Mary Ann Benson
Music for *O Dío Ayuto Noy* and *Una Va Pasada* composed by Nancie Kester

© Calicanto Associates
1995
Second Edition

ISBN 0-9648362-2-X

Orders and inquiries should be directed to the publisher:

Calicanto Associates
6416 Valley View Road
Oakland, CA 94611
510-339-2081

ACKNOWLEDGEMENTS

The authors would like to thank:

The Organization of American Kodály Educators for a grant to begin this project.
The Northern California Association of Kodály Educators for continuing support.
Eleanor G. Locke for her wide background of knowledge, her interest and her commitment to this project.
Holy Names College for the Kodály Music Education program which trained and inspired the four authors.
The Oakland Museum for support during the formative stages.
The Bancroft Library of U.C. Berkeley for their comprehensive collection of reference books on California History.
The authors' families who have heard California History songs for the past ten years.
The students in our classrooms who tested these songs as they learned about the history of our state.

Credits

"Acorn Song, Huchnom" and "Karok Dancing Song" from Stephen Powers, <u>Tribes of California</u>, 1976, copyright The Regents of the University of California. Used with permission.

"Acorn Dance Song" from sampler tape of California Indian music, Phoebe Hearst Museum of Anthropology, The University of California, Berkeley. Used with permission.

"Cloud Woman Tale" excerpt adapted from Indian Tales by Jaime de Angulo, copyright 1953 by A. A. Wyn, Inc. Copyright renewed 1989 by Gui de Angulo. Used by arrangement with Hill and Wang, a division of Farrar, Straus & Giroux, Inc. This material is intended for use by teachers and students in a classroom setting only. For performance rights to this material please contact Hill and Wang, Publisher.

"A Gust of Fall Wind" used with the permission of Silver Burdett Company.

"Whoa Ha Buck" and "On the Road to California" from Austin and Alta Fife, <u>Cowboy and Western Songs: A Comprehensive Anthology</u>, published by Clarkson N. Potter, Inc., 1969, and republished by Creative Concepts Publishing Co., 1993. Used with permission.

INTRODUCTION

They Came Singing: Songs from California's History is a collection of over sixty traditional songs set in an historical context. Throughout California's colorful history, music has played an important part in the lives of her diverse people. The book opens with songs of Native California tribes and continues through European exploration, Spanish and Mexican rule, U.S. exploration and statehood, and songs of the Gold Rush. A second volume beginning with the transcontinental railroad is in the planning stages.

This collection has been tested both in teacher workshops and in elementary school classrooms. The songs may be sung unaccompanied or with guitar, banjo or autoharp. Some of the more boisterous sea shanties may be enriched with accordion or concertina. Several of the songs have easy instructions for games or dances   Two plays are also included. If you wish to create your own play or musical, the possibilities are endless. A Gold Rush program with prospectors carrying picks and pans, or a sea shanty musical with sailors hauling their lines could be great fun to perform.

Since music provides a direct emotional link to the past, these songs will help the singers relive the experiences and feelings of early Californians. The book will appeal to anyone who wishes to know more about California's history through the voice of its people – folk song. *They Came Singing* will enhance the study of California history at any level from elementary school through college and adulthood.

This exciting book is a welcome addition to the multi-cultural study of California History in homes, schools, libraries, museums, and historical societies. It will be of interest to teachers, folk singers and the general public throughout California and the West. We hope you enjoy this book as much as we have enjoyed collecting the songs!

The Authors

CONTENTS

"It is more vital to
feel history than to
memorize its details."

Henrik Van Loon

MUSIC
OF THE
FIRST
PEOPLE

INDIAN TRIBES OF CALIFORNIA

Tolowa
Karok
Modoc
Yurok
Shastan
Achumawi
Hupa
Chimariko
Atsugewi
Wiyot
Wintun
Yana
Northern Paiute
Mattole
Wailaki
Sinkyone
Yuki
Huchnom
Maidu
Washo
Pomo
Patwin
Wappo
Coast Miwok
Miwok
Mono
Costanoan
Koso
Yokuts
Esselen
Tübatulabal
Salinan
Kawaiisu
Chemehuevi
Chumash
Serrano
Mojave
Gabrielino
Halchidhoma
Luiseño
Cahuilla
Kamia
Yuma
Diegueño

N

6

MUSIC OF THE FIRST PEOPLE

The sounds of singing and dancing have risen from the northern wood lands, the slopes of the Sierras, the great Central Valley and the hot Mojave Desert for over 10,000 years. The First People lived in tribes and spoke many different languages. They lived together in relative peace and stability for thousands of years.

California tribal music, like that of all Native American music, is predominately vocal. Words for the songs are simple and repetitive. Often they are sung to syllables called vocables which have no exact meaning. The melodies are of small range and usually pentatonic (five tone scale). The singing style is relaxed. In California, songs and dances might be accompanied by clapper sticks, flutes, various types of rattles or log foot drums.

Spanish and Anglo conquest in the nineteenth century changed forever the Indian way of life; but many tribes continued to preserve and recreate their traditional culture in new settings. Music is passed from generation to generation by ear and imitation like basket-making, cooking or woodworking.

Today the majority of California Indians live in the cities. They gather at pow-wows and festivals to celebrate pride in identity and joy in being together. Trained singers and dancers come from tribal homelands in many parts of the state to perform, compete, and share their art with the general public.

The ancestors lived as hunter-gatherers, and sang of the spirit world, healing and living closely with nature. Songs gave power to the favorite pastime of group gambling. All important activities in ancient tribal life had their songs. Many hundreds, forgotten by modern singers, have been preserved on tapes by scholars who went to oldtimers to record over the past century.

California's First People still continue a musical tradition which adds to the rich mosaic of our cultural history.

Clapper Stick

ACORN SONGS

Acorns were an important part of the diet of Native Californians. Acorn preparation consisted of gathering, cracking open the shells, skinning, grinding, leaching out the poisonous tannin, soaking for several hours, and then cooking the meal into an acorn mush. The laborious work of grinding meal was often accompanied by songs sung to the rhythm of a pestle pounding into a shallow stone mortar.

Acorn Song
Wehichit Yokuts

Ancient tales tell us that in the old days the tribal people carried slightly hollowed grinding stones. The wise Coyote suggested that they use stationary granite boulders instead. Women would gather at these boulders to grind their acorns and sing. Many of these resulting grinding holes are still visible today.

Hay way na wo lay ya korn hay pa ra no wa ma yen

Acorn Song
Huchnom

The Huchnom Indians mixed the red earth from the Potter Valley into their acorn bread, which added sweetness and extended the acorn meal.

Ya- ah hay - lay ya - no hee - lo, ya - ah hay - lay ya - no hee - lo, ya-

a hay - lay ya - no hee - lo, lee - mo hay - lay ya - lo hee - lo.

Acorn Dance
Sierra Miwok

The Acorn Dance Song celebrated the acorn harvest in the fall of each year. Ceremonial dancers wore costumes representing significant spirits or animals. It began with three days of fasting. On the fourth day, selected women prepared acorn mush and other food for the feast. When the food was ready, everyone began to move slowly around the fire in a big circle, chanting and shaking rattles over the flames. The dance ended when one of the women spread acorn mush around the fire in four directions so that it might be carried into the air and eaten by the spirits of the dead. Until this was done, no one ate anything. After the feast, there was dancing well into the night.

Dance Directions: Inner and outer circles are formed with participants facing one another. The two circles rotate in opposite directions as participants side-step slowly to the beat of the music. The song may be enhanced by shaking a rattle on the first and fourth beat of every measure.

Stone Mortar and Pestle

DANCES and CEREMONIALS

Ceremonial dancing had great religious significance and was also an important part of tribal social life. Dances were performed in round houses or out of doors. Many of the old round houses are now being restored as tribal elders revive the traditional dances in their communities.

Gourd Rattles

Dance Whistle

Tolowa Dance Costume

Ceremonial Dance Song
Tolowa

This ceremonial dance from the Tolowa world renewal ceremony was performed at the end of summer. A circle was formed around a fire with the dancers on one side and spectators on the other. Male dancers wore elaborate feather headdresses. Female dancers wore dresses decorated with abalone shells which provided rhythmic accompaniment.

Ha   way   ha   way   ha - ah   way   ha   way,

Ha   way   ha   way   ha - ah   way   ha!

Dancing Song
Karok

This dance was performed in early autumn by elaborately costumed men, dancing slowly in a long line. All members of the Karok tribe were present, plus neighboring tribes along the Klamath River. The ceremony was called *sif-san-di pik-i-a-vish*, which means "working the earth." The purpose was to pacify spirits of earth and forest in order to prevent forest fires, landslides, earthquakes, and droughts. No one was allowed to take a salmon until ten days after the ceremony.

Hee- no way   no- hee-no   o- hee no,   Hee no way   o-hee no   no- hee no,

Hee- no way   no- hee-no   o-hee no,   Hee no way   o-hee- no   no- hee no.

11

Bird Dance Song
Mojave

The Mojave people still live on their ancient lands along the Colorado River which separates California from Arizona. Among the Southern California tribes, there is a series of Bird Songs which are performed during times of celebration. The songs describe the lives and migrations of actual birds. Typical of these is the Mojave Bird Dance, an ancient form of dance and song.

Ha ah cha lee-wa-lee-wa ha cha ko-mo-ko ma ha

cha lee-wa-lee-wa Ha ah cha lee-wa-lee wa ha

cha ko-mo-ko ma ha cha lee-wa-lee wa, ha cha ko-mo-ko ma.

Dance Directions: Boys and girls form separate lines, facing each other.

Section A: Using a shuffling two step (step-close), dancers take three steps forward, then two steps backward. Repeat

Section B: Dancers take five steps forward, turning on the fifth step to face the other line. During this action, they have traded places.

Repeat dance to return to original places.
In this dance, rattles may be used for percussive effects.

Snowflake Song
Mono Paiute

The singer welcomes the first snow of winter in the high Sierra.

T'a nee tsee na ah na ma ma no ho - pen, t'a

nee tsee ta nay tna a na ma ma no ho - pen.

Mahogany Tree Song
Tache Yokuts

Sturdy digging sticks were needed for such food staples as roots and bulbs, and the mahogany tree in the Sierra foothills furnished the best sticks. When early settlers saw the natives digging for food, they called them "Digger" Indians as if it were the name of a tribe. Non-native people did not understand the hunter-gatherer way of life. The word for mahogany tree is *ote-sigh*. *No-too-nay* means go up in the mountains. The free translation of the song is: "Mahogany tree sings about himself. I will go up in the mountains, and go along the mountains."

Ote-sigh ya na way hay, Ote - sigh ya na ha way,

No too na a dee lay hay nen, Ote-sigh ya na ha way.

Cloud Song
Achumawi

This song comes from the Achumawi People of the Pit River and means, "I am a female cloud.
I come covering the sky."

Ah loo ta ha goo - tsi ah say - la wa sa na ah

say la wa sa na ah loo - ta - ha goo - tsi

14

Cloud Maiden Tale

CAST: Narrator #1,
                         Narrator #2,
                         Silver Fox
                         Frog Woman
                         Cloud Woman
                         Eagle Woman
                         Chorus of students
                         Two cloud holders
                         Instrumentalists

COSTUMES: Silver Fox: Silver fox mask
                   Frog Woman: Frog mask.
                   Cloud Woman: White gown, Native American jewelry, and
                       moccasins.
                   Eagle Woman: Eagle mask and with cardboard eagle wings and
                       black or grey leotard.

SPECIAL EFFECTS: Cardboard in the shape of a white cloud held by students.
                   Rain: rain stick, rattle, cymbal and brush.
                   Water: sandblocks, glockenspiels, metallaphone
                   Masks: Silver Fox, Frog Woman, Eagle Woman
                   Clouds: paper cloud shapes, decorated, cloud headband masks
                   Rocks: covered boxes to simulate rocks.

Eagle Woman

Frog Woman

Silver Fox

NARRATOR #1: Today we are acting out a story told in the style of the Achumawi people of the Pit River in Northern California. It is part of a long story about a trip from the mountains down to the coast. It can be found in the book *Indian Tales* by Jaime de Angulo.

Jaime de Angulo lived among the Pit River people for forty years. He was a doctor, anthropologist, philosopher, musician and poet. His knowledge of the myths and tales of the Achumawi people led him to write them down for his own children in the form of a fictional journey. The time period is pre-history, when native people felt there was a strong connection between animals and humans. The characters are Silver Fox, Frog Woman, Cloud Maiden and Eagle Woman. Coyote, mentioned by Silver Fox, is both creator and prankster in Indian lore.

NARRATOR #2: One day Silver Fox and Frog Woman noticed a cloud hovering far away near the horizon. It had a strange shape, and they wondered what it was and why it looked like that. They watched it for a long time until they went to sleep.

CHORUS holding individual clouds sings CLOUD SONG. SILVER FOX and FROG WOMAN look at the cloud questioningly while the song is being sung. Then they curl up on the floor and pretend to sleep. The clouds fill the stage and the song gets gradually softer, fading to the end.

NARRATOR #2: When they woke up, the cloud had covered all the sky, and Silver Fox and Frog Woman heard somebody singing in the cloud. It sounded like a young woman's voice but they couldn't see anyone up there.

CLOUD WOMAN sings CLOUD SONG either by herself or with a few other voices joining in. She is hidden behind the cloud.

FROG WOMAN *(speaking to Silver Fox):* It sounds as if someone said, "I am a woman cloud. I am the mother of water." That means it's going to rain! You are the cause of that! You dreamed it on purpose!

SILVER FOX smiles slyly at FROG WOMAN but says nothing

NARRATOR #2: Soon it started to rain. SILVER FOX and FROG WOMAN found a cave in the rocks and went to sleep inside.

SILVER FOX and FROG WOMAN lie down and pretend to sleep.
Rain sound effects continue.

NARRATOR #2: When they came out again, the rain had stopped and there was a
        spring of water gurgling out of the rocks.

Water sound effects

SILVER FOX: There is the water that Coyote wanted.

CLOUD WOMAN appeasrs, singing her song, and sits down on a rock. Water sound
continues quietly.

SILVER FOX and FROG WOMAN to CLOUD WOMAN:
        Are you the one who was singing in the cloud?

CLOUD WOMAN: Yes, I am the one.

SILVER FOX and FROG WOMAN:
        Have you come down to live with us?

CLOUD WOMAN: No, I am a person of the air. I cannot live with you. I must go back
        to where I belong, but I took pity on you because you were thirsty
        and the earth is thirsty. Somebody sent me.

SILVER FOX: Who sent you?

CLOUD WOMAN: The same one who makes sounds in our heads, the one who makes
        words. Now I have to go. My name is Aluta, but when I travel
        through the air I am Lawiidza.

CLOUD WOMAN disappears behind the cloud singing her song.

NARRATOR #2: Then Silver Fox and Frog Woman saw she was an Eagle Woman
        and she flew away.

EAGLE WOMAN appears from behind the cloud, spreads her wings and appears to fly
away. CHORUS sings CLOUD SONG repeating it three more times.

HAND GAME SONGS

Hand games have always been popular pastimes of Native Californians and vary only slightly from one tribe to another. Teams are chosen and before the game begins each side offers something of value which must be matched by the other side. When the stake is large enough to be worthwhile, the game begins.

To play the games, designated players on one team hide a marked and unmarked bone in their hands. The other side must guess where the marked bone is located. Scoring is based on various combinations. Players have a set of gambling songs which are said to bring luck or power. Gambling games are well attended and may go on all day and well into the night.

Two Hand Game Songs
Sierra Miwok

These two chants are typical of Miwok hand game songs. Such songs are repeated over and over and changed when desired. The purpose of the songs is to trick the opposing side into listening, thus losing their concentration. The Miwok refer to the marked bone as woman and the unmarked bone as man.

18

Grass Game Song
Pomo

Grass game is another term for bone hand games. In this version players hide bones rolled in dried grass in their hands. The marked bone is called *tep*, and the unmarked bone *wi*.

Moderate

Ha - nee   a - nee   no - o   way   ha - nee yeh   ha - nee yeh

Ha - nee   a - nee   no - o   way   ha - nee yeh   ha - nee yeh

Materials needed:

Four "bones" approximately two inches long and one inch wide can be made from wooden dowels. Two are plain and two are marked with rings of wire or strings tied around the middle. The players need to be able to feel the marked bone in their hand. Indians used bones from the leg of a deer or other animal, and occasionally wood.

Ten to twelve counting sticks are used to keep score. These sticks are about 12 inches long and are made from either thin wooden dowels or peeled wood . Indian sticks are pointed at one end.

Two pieces of cloth (or bandanas) can be used by the players to conceal the bones.

Bone game instructions:

Two teams sit facing one another. Each has its own gambling song. The first team chooses two players who are each given a marked and unmarked bone. Two guessers are chosen from the opposite team. A score keeper for each team keeps track of the counting sticks, which are evenly divided.

The first team sings its gambling song as the players hide the bones in their hands under a cloth on their laps. Then the players hold their closed hands in front of their chests, rotating their hands and by their actions trying to confuse the viewer.

When ready, the players hold out their hands. The guessers from the other side point clearly left or right to signify which hand holds the marked bone. If both guesses are incorrect, players keep the bones for another round and their team receives two counters. If both guesses are correct, the other side gets a turn and the losing side forfeits two sticks. If one guess is correct and the other incorrect, no sticks are exchanged and the other side gets a turn. When all the counters have been won over to one side, the game is ended. The Miwok version uses ten counters and the Pomo version uses twelve.

ROUTES OF
CALIFORNIA EXPLORERS

Southern Oregon

Coquille River

Drake's Voyage in 1579 ⎯ ⎯ →

Viscaino's Voyage in 1602 ⎯ ‥ ⎯ ‥ →

Portolá's Expedition in 1769

Overland ⋯⋯⋯⋯⋯ →

Ships ⎯ ⎯ ⎯ ⎯ →

Anza's Overland Route in 1774 ⎯ ‥ ⎯ ‥

Drake's Bay

San Francisco Bay

Monterey Bay

CALIFORNIA

Colorado River

Drake's route home

San Diego Bay

present U.S.-Mexican border

MEXICO

Tubac

Altar

BAJA
CALIFORNIA

Loreto

La Paz

San Blas

Pacific Ocean

Acapulco

N
W   E
S

NK

SONGS
OF THE
EARLY
EXPLORERS

EXPLORATIONS IN EARLY CALIFORNIA

1492   COLUMBUS searched for routes from Spain to Asia. Instead, he landed in San Salvador, West Indies.

1500   •

1519   MAGELLAN attempted to find a passage through South America. He sailed around tip of South America (through the "Straits of Magellan") and on to the Philippines where he was killed. His ship sailed back to Spain—the first ship to sail around the world. Trade began between Spain and the Philippines. (See Manila Galleons, pg. 23.)

1535   CORTES searched for gold north from Mexico and found Baja California.

1536   CABEZA DE VACA led a land expedition from Florida to Mexico. Indians told of treasure in the north.

1539   ULLOA led three ships looking for gold and passage to Atlantic Ocean (the mythical Straits of Anion) instead discovered that Baja California was a peninsula, not an island.

1540   CABRILLO landed in San Diego Bay, the first European to reach Alta California. After his death, his crew continued up the Oregon coast looking for a passage to the Atlantic.

1565   MANILA GALLEONS sailed back to Mexico from the Philippines via Northern California to catch the favorable trade winds.

1578   CERMENO searched for a harbor in Alta California and crashed in Drakes Bay.

1579   DRAKE sailed up the California coast.

1600   •

1602   VISCAINO led an exploration party to find harbors for Spanish Galleons. Along the way he named San Diego Bay, Santa Catalina Island, Santa Barbara Channel and located a suitable harbor in Monterey Bay.

1602-1768 No explorations occured in Alta California

1700   •

1768   GALVEZ sent missionaries and soldiers to Alta California to discover a land route in order to build Missions.

1769   PORTOLA AND FATHER SERRA founded missions and established a land route. They founded the city of San Diego, arrived at Monterey Bay and discovered San Francisco Bay.

1770   FATHER SERRA continued to establish missions in Alta California and wanted families to settle the land.

1774   ANZA led settlers from Sonora Mexico across deserts and mountains to San Gabriel Mission. He founded the Presidio at San Francisco.

1776-1781 The cities of San Francisco, San Jose and Los Angeles were founded.

SONGS OF THE EARLY EXPLORERS

The Spanish and English explorers who reached North and South America did not have an easy time on their voyages. Ships were away from land for months and frequently years at a time. Venturing into the unknown required stamina, courage and faith. Regularity of schedule, ritual and song were sources of comfort for the sailors on their long voyages. Food and water often ran out and sailors died from thirst and starvation. Rats ran wild on the ships and sanitation was very poor. Many sailors died of various diseases, particulary scurvy, caused by lack of vitamin C. There was much heavy work to do aboard ship (e.g. raising large sails and hauling thick lines). Explorers and seafarers often sang to make their work seem easier and to help them haul on a regular beat.

SPANISH EXPLORERS

Reports of Christopher Columbus's voyage to the New World in 1492 interested other countries in the possibility of finding gold, silver and other riches. For many years, however, Spain was the only country to pursue exploration of Mexico and California. In 1519 the discovery of the Straits of Magellan off the coast of South America opened up Spanish trade between New Spain (Mexico) and the Philippines. On the return voyage from the Philippines, the Spanish trade ships (Manila Galleons) frequently sailed near the coast of California to avoid tradewinds pulling them eastward. The crews of these ships often sighted the rugged California coast as they made their journeys back to Mexico.

In 1542 Captain Juan Rodriguez Cabrillo and his crew were the first Europeans to land in Alta California (our present California). They landed at San Diego Bay and then made their way up the coast naming and claiming lands for Spain. In 1602, Captain Sebastian Vizcaino charted the California coast and informed the Viceroy of New Spain that Monterey would provide a good harbor. However, the Viceroy decided against further exploration because of the danger and high expense of the long voyages. For more than 160 years no Spanish ships sailed into Alta California.

ENGLISH EXPLORERS

Captain Francis Drake came to the New World in search of wealth. In 1579, Drake sailed his ship, "The Golden Hind" up the California Coast, looking for the illusive Northwest Passage (Strait of Anian) before his return to England. He anchored in a bay thirty miles north of San Francisco, which he named New Albion and claimed for England. If the native people had not been exposed to European music during the Spanish voyages to California, they certainly were during Drake's visit. Drake and his crew, which included musicians, were said to have sung extensively on their voyage from England to California.

Una Va Pasada

Sailors did not have clocks aboard ship until the late 16th century. They relied upon a half-hour glass *(ampolleta)* filled with sand. It was turned over every 30 minutes when the sand emptied. The sailors regulated this sand clock with the use of a sun dial at noontime. At night, the navigators could tell time by observing the position of the stars. A young sailor would turn the *ampolleta* and sing *"Una va pasada, y en dos muele,"* ("One glass is gone and now the second flows"). Then he would call to the forward lookout, *"Ah! de proa alerta, buena guardia!"* ("Hey, you! Forward, look alive, keep good watch!") At this point, the lookout was to shout or grunt to show that he was indeed awake. Because the music was not available for this song and *O Dío, Ayuta Noy*, Nancie Kester wrote the melodies based on an authentic text.

U - na va pa - sa - da. Y en dos mue - le.
One glass is o - ver, Now the se - cond flow - eth.

Más mo - le - rá, si mi Diós guer - rá, a mi Diós pi - da - mos,
More shall run through if it is God's will. O Lord, let us pray.

que bien vi - a pa - ga - mos, - yá la que es,
Keep our voy - age safe, through our bles - sed

Ma - dre de Diós, y a - bo - ga - da nues - tra,
Moth - er of God, our ad - vo - cate on high, (Pro) -

que nos li - bre de a - gua de bom - ba y tor - men - ta.
tect us from all dan - ger and send no tem - pest nigh.

O Dío Ayuta Noy

Early Spanish explorers were formal and ritualistic as they tended to their duties aboard ship. The change of the person in charge of the helm (wheel or tiller) and the change of the watch (overseeing the ship and its course) were always semi-religious rituals, observed with beauty and serenity. These events reminded the mariners every half-hour (when the sand had run through the *ampolleta*) that their safety depended not only upon their skill, but also upon the grace of God.

This traditional Spanish *Saloma* (shanty) dates back to the early explorers. The shanty man sang the first half of each line and the men hauled on the "O" and joined in on the second half while they got a new hold on the halyard.

High Barbary

High Barbary was a popular English sea song of the late sixteenth century. It might well have been sung by Drake's crew as they looted Mexican towns and captured the treasure-laden returning Manila Galleons, all in the name of the English Queen, Elizabeth I.

Look a - head, look a- stern, look a - wea - ther and a
lee, Blow high, blow low, and so sail - ed
we. I see a wreck to wind –ward and a lof - ty ship to
lee. A- sail - ing down all on the coasts of High Bar - bar - y.

2. "O are you a pirate or a man o' war?" cried we.
   "O no! I' m not a pirate, but a man o' war," cried he.

3. "Then back up your tops' ls* and heave your vessel to,
   For we have got some letters to be carried home by you."

4. "We'll back up our tops' ls and heave our vessel to;
   But only in some harbour and along the side of you."

5. For broadside, for broadside, they fought all on the main;
   Until at last the frigate shot the pirate' s mast away.

6. "For quarter, for quarter!" the saucy pirate cried.
   The quarter that we showed them was to sink them in the tide.

7. With cutlass and gun, o, we fought for hours three;
   The ship it was their coffin, and their grave it was the sea.

*Topsails

26

Haul on the Bowlin'

The English had a habit of singing out on board ship. Sailors sang certain words or phrases (e.g. "Way hey or Hee lee") while performing specific tasks on ship or on shore. Work songs aboard English ships were later called sea shanties.

This is a variant of the oldest known British short-haul shanty, believed to go back to the time of Henry VIII. The pull is performed on the last "Haul!" of each verse.

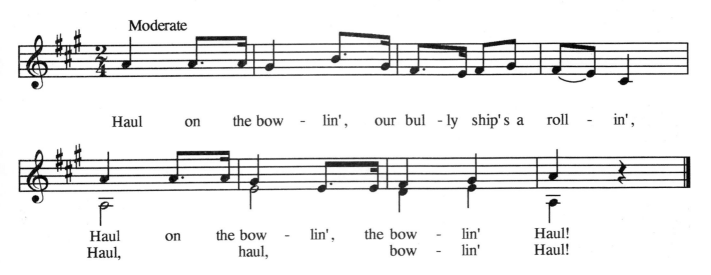

Haul   on   the bow - lin',   our bul - ly ship's a   roll - in',

Haul   on   the bow - lin',   the bow - lin'   Haul!
Haul,   haul,   bow - lin'   Haul!

2. Haul on the bowlin' so early in the mornin'.

3. Haul on the bowlin', we'll hang for finer weather.

4. Haul on the bowlin', the bonny, bonny bowlin'.

Drake's Ship, "The Golden Hind"

Evening Prayer
for Thursday, July 5, 1579

Before Sir Francis Drake and his crew landed in Northern California, they were fearful that they might meet unfriendly Indians. The English crew knew from past voyages that the native peoples of South America hated the Spanish and they feared what might happen if the North American people mistook their ship for a Spanish vessel. When his ship, the Golden Hind, landed in California, Drake must have been surprised and relieved for the crew was met by Miwok people, whom Drake described as "courteous and showing interest in the strange European music." When Drake arrived in what is now Marin County on July 5, 1579, he and his men might have sung this prayer.

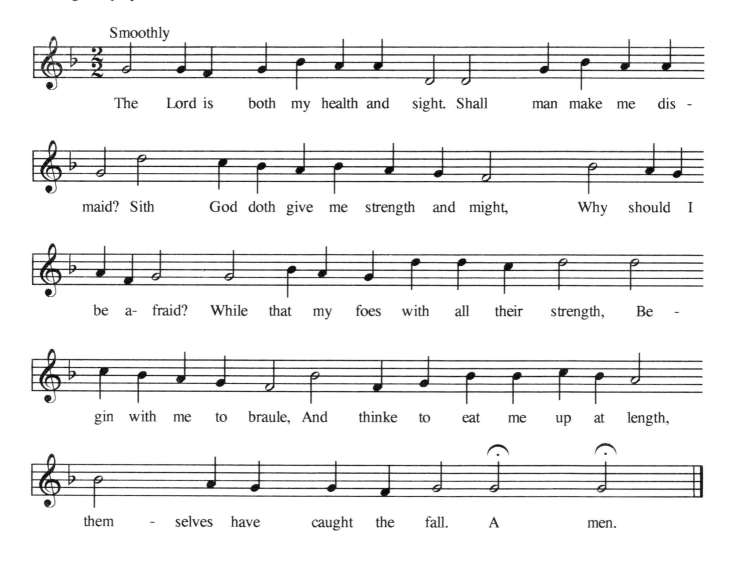

The Lord is both my health and sight. Shall man make me dis-maid? Sith God doth give me strength and might, Why should I be a-fraid? While that my foes with all their strength, Be-gin with me to braule, And thinke to eat me up at length, them-selves have caught the fall. A men.

SPANISH MISSION SONGS

MISSIONS OF CALIFORNIA

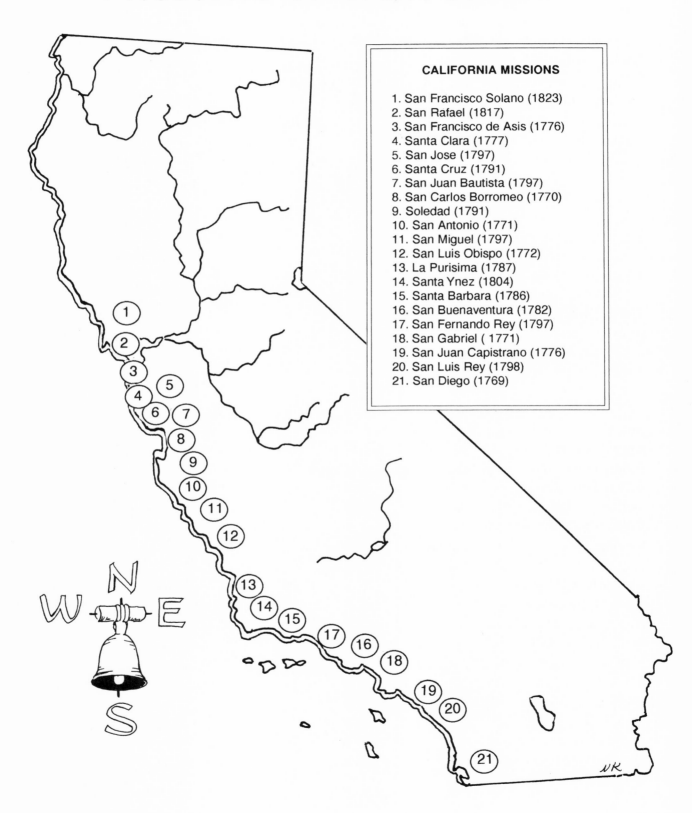

CALIFORNIA MISSIONS

1. San Francisco Solano (1823)
2. San Rafael (1817)
3. San Francisco de Asis (1776)
4. Santa Clara (1777)
5. San Jose (1797)
6. Santa Cruz (1791)
7. San Juan Bautista (1797)
8. San Carlos Borromeo (1770)
9. Soledad (1791)
10. San Antonio (1771)
11. San Miguel (1797)
12. San Luis Obispo (1772)
13. La Purisima (1787)
14. Santa Ynez (1804)
15. Santa Barbara (1786)
16. San Buenaventura (1782)
17. San Fernando Rey (1797)
18. San Gabriel (1771)
19. San Juan Capistrano (1776)
20. San Luis Rey (1798)
21. San Diego (1769)

SPANISH MISSION SONGS

As we travel northward from San Diego to Sonoma, the beautiful old mission buildings that dot the landscape remind us of the earliest days of Spanish settlement. Late in the eighteenth century, with the English and Russians showing great interest in the area, Spain decided to colonize Alta California. A chain of missions was proposed with accompanying presidios to protect them. Don Gaspar de Portola, a former governor of Baja California, and Father Junipero Serra, a Franciscan monk, were chosen to implement the plan. The first California mission and presidio were founded at San Diego in 1769.

The Franciscan fathers felt it was their sacred duty to educate and convert the native people to Christianity. The mission Indians were taught Spanish and forced to adopt the culture of Spain. Unfortunately, in the process, old tribal customs and languages were lost. Equally devastating, however, was the native people's lack of immunity to European diseases. Common childhood illnesses such as measles carried off large numbers of mission Indians.

The mission period was brief, lasting only fifty years. By 1823 twenty-one missions, each a day's journey from the next, had been founded along El Camino Real; but by this time, Spain's power was waning. One after another, her colonies seceded. In 1821, New Spain broke away and became the Republic of Mexico. It was the beginning of the end for the mission system in California.

Music was a natural part of the religious and secular life at the missions. At first all church singing was performed by the congregation, which consisted primarily of native people. Later formal choirs were organized. Following European tradition, choir membership was open only to boys showing musical talent. They were taught to read music and play instruments as well as to sing and chant. Many of the most influential padres were fine musicians. Father Serra, who had been a boy soprano, was inspired to become a priest as a result of his musical training.

European style instruments were made by native craftspeople. These were designed with ingenuity, including flutes made from rifle barrels and violins with ornately carved scrolls representing horses and other creatures. The huge mission bells, imported from Mexico and Peru, played an important role in announcing events at the mission such as feasts, visitors, impending danger or death. Barrel organs were eventually introduced, opening up further musical possibilities. The first organ was a gift from the English sea Captain, George Vancouver in 1793.

Secular music was a part of mission life also. Love songs, children's songs and dance music, brought by the accompanying soldiers and settlers, were an integral part of the musical scene.

El Cántico del Alba

This song and its musical companion, *Alabado*, were heard everywhere in Spanish California. Many of the Spanish padres were musicians and they taught the indians how to read music, make musical instruments, and play in an orchestra. Because California natives were a musical people, this was one of the more enjoyable aspects of the Mission Period. These two songs should either be sung a cappella (unaccompanied) or with hand bells or tone chimes as notated.

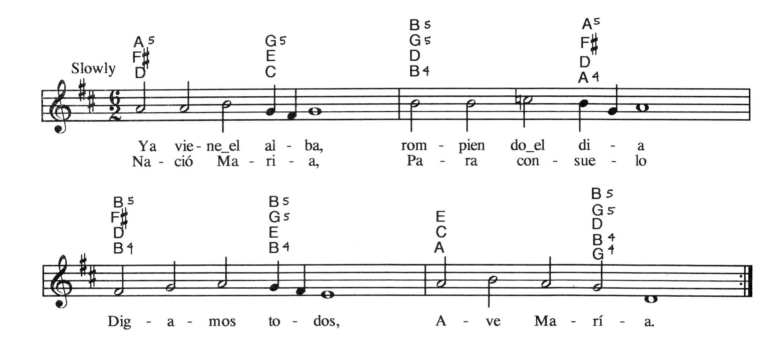

Ya vie-ne el al - ba, rom - pien do el di - a
Na - ció Ma - ri - a, Pa - ra con - sue - lo

Dig - a - mos to - dos, A - ve Ma - rí - a.

Singable translation:

Now comes the dawning day, gilding the morning sky, Lift up your voice to pray "Ave Maria".
Mother, to earth you came, easing our sorrows, Softly we call your name, "Ave María".

Suggestions for Performance

Bells needed: G4, A 4, B4, C5, D5, E5, F#5, G5, A5, B5

Introduction: A5, B5, A5, G5, D5

Suggested Tone sets. Each performer can easily play two bells in the following pairs.:

D5 F#5   C5 E5   A4 A5   B4 G5   G4 B5

Alabado

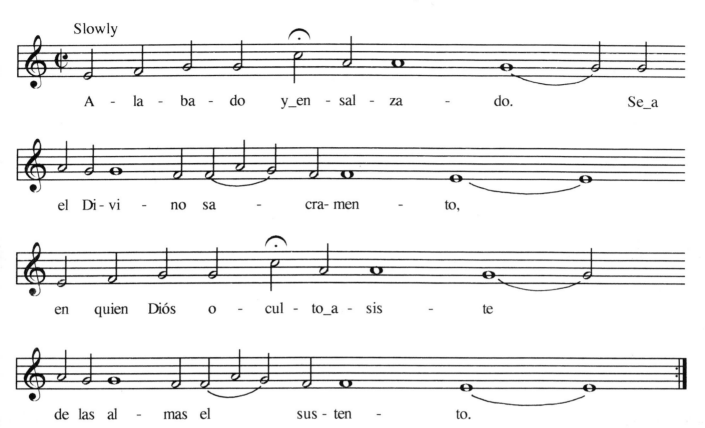

Slowly

A - la - ba - do y_en - sal - za - do. Se_a

el Di - vi - no sa - cra - men - to,

en quien Diós o - cul - to_a - sis - te

de las al - mas el sus - ten - to.

Translation:
Lift your heart in joy and exalt him
In the blessed Sacrament all Holy,
Where He, the Lord, His glory veiling
Comforts souls, true and lowly.

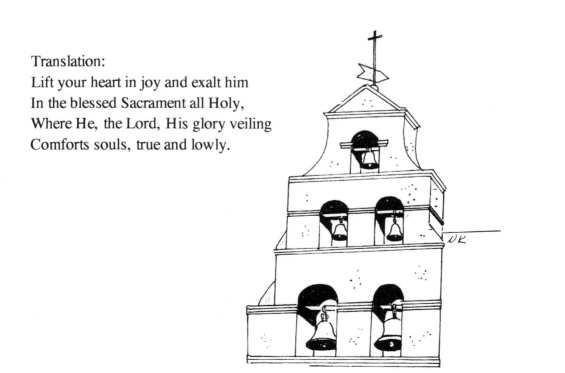

33

Santa Barbara Folk Song

This song is attributed to Padre Narciso Duran, of the San Jose Mission, who was an accomplished musician, teacher, and composer. In his mission, Padre Duran had a chorus of 30 members and an orchestra, which included violins, flutes, trumpets and drums. He also developed a music notation system to help his choir read music. Native people would walk for miles to hear one of the mission's concerts. Padre Duran was at the San Jose mission for 27 years before becoming Father President of the California Mission system.

Li - ber - tad, li - ber - tad sac - ro San - to, Pues por
Grant me free - dom O Ho - ly Spi - rit. It is

siem - pre mi nu - men se - rás; Me ver me
you that I ev - er a - dore. Let me

reis pe - re - cer en tus ar - ras. Mas vi -
come to my end in your gra - ces, and

vir en pri - sio - nes ja - más.
live as a priso - ner no more.

El Quelelé

Some of the Presidio Soldiers brought their families along. *El Quelelé* (The White Hawk) might well have been sung by children in Spanish California.

El Que - le - lé se mu - rió, ay, ay, ay, ay, ay!
Pa - pa Que - le - lé has died,

A las trés de la ma - ña na.
Died as the morn - ing was break - ing.

El Que - le - lé se mu - rió, ay, ay, ay, ay, ay!
Pa - pa Que - le - lé has died,

Y lo lle - van a_en - ter - rar.
Now to his grave he must go.

Tres dra - go - nes y_un ca bo, Ay, ay, ay, ay, ay, ay!
Three dra - goons and a corp' - ral,

Y_el ga - to de sac - ris - tán.
Tom cat for sac - ris - tan, too,

Y los Que - lé - les chi - qui - tos, Ay, ay, ay, ay, ay, ay!
And all the ba - by Que - le - lés,

Ya se mu - rian de llo - rar.
Cry them to death in their woe.

35

Pronunciation Guide for Spanish Songs

a = ah

e = as in "pen or a as in "day"

i = ee

o = oh

u = oo

ll = ly as in "million"

y (alone) = ee

y (with vowel) = as in "yes"

ñ = ny as in "canyon"

r = rolled with a slight "d" sound

rr = strong rolled sound

v = almost a "b" sound

 *In the Spanish language, when a word ends in a vowel and the next word begins with a vowel, the two vowels are joined together as one sound. This is called an elision.

SONGS
OF THE
MEXICAN
RANCHO
PERIOD

CALIFORNIA RANCHOS

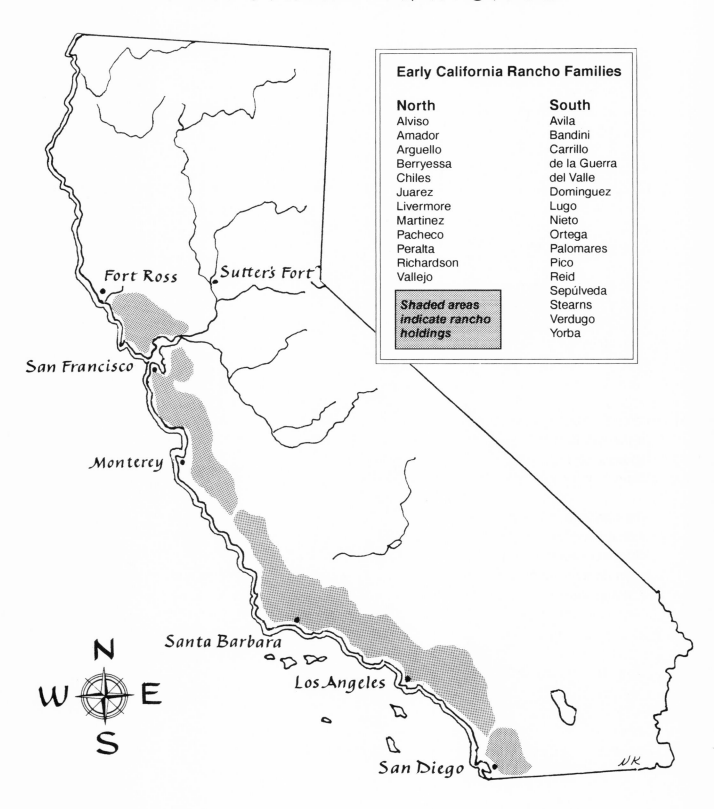

Fort Ross

Sutter's Fort

San Francisco

Monterey

Santa Barbara

Los Angeles

San Diego

N
W • E
S

Early California Rancho Families

North	South
Alviso	Avila
Amador	Bandini
Arguello	Carrillo
Berryessa	de la Guerra
Chiles	del Valle
Juarez	Dominguez
Livermore	Lugo
Martinez	Nieto
Pacheco	Ortega
Peralta	Palomares
Richardson	Pico
Vallejo	Reid
	Sepúlveda
	Stearns
	Verdugo
	Yorba

Shaded areas indicate rancho holdings

NK

SONGS OF THE
MEXICAN RANCHO PERIOD

Pico, Sepulveda, Vallejo, Noriega, Peralta -- the names of the great ranchos and their owners are echoed throughout California in town, street and place names. Nearly every town or city in the middle and southern coastal regions of the state was once part of some old Rancho.

In 1822 Mexico won its independence from Spain. California was now a province of Mexico and the government divided the huge mission holdings and made the land available to its citizens. During the years of Mexican rule, 1822 to 1848, many new ranchos were created. The mild California climate and rich grazing land contributed toward making this a period of great prosperity.

Each rancho became a self-contained community with its own artisans, blacksmiths, stables, corrals and vegetable gardens. Whatever could not be produced on site was obtained by trading hides and tallow for goods brought by foreign ships. So important were hides to California's economy that they became known as "California bank notes."

The ranchero and his family lived in a large adobe *casa* or main house. Their activities centered around the ranch and the family and the pace of living was relaxed. The men were noted for their superb horsemanship and it was common for them to spend the entire day in the saddle riding the golden, rolling hills of their vast ranchlands. The many Indian laborers kept things running, doing the work of *vaqueros* (cowhands), artisans, farm laborers and domestic servants in exchange for food, clothing, and a place to live.

The *Californios* (as the rancheros called themselves) had a talent and a taste for music. In almost every family there were those who could play the *vihuela* (guitar), violin or flute. They were noted for their love of parties and festivity and evenings at the *hacienda*s were taken up with singing, dancing and games. A special occasion such as a holiday, rodeo or wedding called for a *fiesta* (celebration) Music and dancing were always the most important part of the festivities. Sometimes dances lasted as long as three days. Some participants would dance all night, sleep three hours after daylight, have a merienda (picnic) in the forenoon and begin dancing again in the afternoon. The big religious holidays had their own special music, customs and celebrations such as the Christmas ceremony of *Las Posadas*.

Many visitors and outside observers have left written accounts of the rich family life, generous hospitality and love of laughter and music of these early Californians.

Las Mañanitas

These two traditional songs date from the days of Spanish rule. These songs of praise to the Virgin of Guadalupe were originally sung at dawn. They gradually evolved into early morning serenades to celebrate the birthday of relatives or dear friends. The two songs, often sung as a pair, are as well-known today as they were during the Rancho period.

Las Mañanitas del Rey David

La Primavera

La Primavera (The Springtime), a song from the Rancho days, celebrates the glories of this season. The mildness of the California climate encouraged outdoor living and the *merienda* (picnic) was a social occasion enjoyed frequently by the *Californios*.

Ya vie- ne la prim- a- ve- ra, sem - bran- do flor- es, sem-
The springtime at last is com- ing so full of flo- wers, so

bran- do flor- es, ay, ay! Y ya los cam- pos se_es- mal- tan, De
full of flo- wers, ay, ay! The fields now in splen - dor brim- ming with

mil co - lo- res, de mil co - lo- res. Can - tan las
ma- ny co- lors, with ma- ny co- lors. Song - birds are

a- ves, can - tan las a- ves. Los o- te- ros re-
sing - ing, voi - ces sweet- ly ring- ing, Echo- ing through the

pi- tan sus tri- nos sua- ves, sus tri- nos suaves.
hill- sides sing - ing of spring – time, sing- ing of spring – time.

42

El Charro

This humorous song from California Rancho days is a tongue in cheek account of a charro (ranch-hand) whose expectations become progressively more unrealistic.

1. Es - ta - ba_un char - ro sen - tan - do en las tran - cas
1. A lone ly cow - punch - er sat brood ing, on the fence of a

de_un cor - ral. 1.Es ral. Su may - or - do - mo le
big cor - ral, A ral, His fore - man ap - proached him and

di - ce, "No_es - tes tris - te, Ni - co - lás."
asked him, "Why so down - cast, Ni - co - lás?"

2. "Necesito un buen caballo, Buena silla y buen gabón." (2X)
   Su mayordomo le dice, "Lo que gustes, Nicolás." (2X)

3. "Y su hija bonita, Maria, Con ella me_hé de casar." (2X)
   Su mayordomo le dice, "Tiene dueño, Nicolás." (2X)

4. Nicolás se desespera, y se quiere desbarrancar (2X)
   Su mayordomo le dice, "De cabeza, Nicolás!" (2X)

2. " I need a horse and a saddle, and an overcoat of wool."(2X)
   Kindly the foreman assured him, "You shall have them, Nicolás." (2X)

3. "And your lovely daughter, Maria, I would like to marry her, too." (2X)
   Firmly the foreman informed him, "She is taken, Nicolás." (2X)

4. The cowboy cried, " If I can't have her, then I'll throw myself off the cliff!" (2X)
   Kindly the foreman suggested, "Then go headfirst, Nicolás!" (2X)

Cielito Lindo

This famous old Mexican song was sung by the *Californios*. It remains as popular today as it was during the time of the Ranchos.

De la Sier - ra Mo - re - na, Cie - li - to Lin - do, vie - nen ba -
From the Sier - ra Mo - re - na, Cie - li - to Lin - do, now they come

jan - do. Un par de_o - ji - tos ne - gros Cie - li - to
sing- ing, With their bril - liant eyes flash ing and their clear

Lin - do de con - tra - ban - do. Ay, ay, ay,
voi - ces joy - fully ring - ing.

ay. Can - ta_y no llo - res, por - que can - tan - do se_a -
Sing, ba nish sad - ness. For lift -ing up your

le - gran, Cie - li - to Lin - do los co - ra - zo - nes.
voice will bring you a heart that's brim - ming with glad - ness.

2. Una flecha_en el aire, Cielito Lindo, lanzó Cupido,
Y como fué jugando, Cielito Lindo_a mi me_ha herido.

2. Cupid playing one morninig, Cielito Lindo, sent arrows flying,
One has wounded me sorely, Cielito Lindo, and left me crying.

44

LAS POSADAS CELEBRATION

Las Posadas is the traditional Mexican custom of celebrating Christmas. *Las Posadas* (the lodgings) represents the several inns at which Joseph begged shelter for Mary. Each evening of the nine days before Christmas, a couple representing Mary and Joseph and a group of villagers go from house to house begging shelter. Finally the head of a house invites the group to enter and join the family in refreshments and dancing. At the end of the evening's fun, the children break the piñata. These next three songs may be used with a Las Posadas play.

Marchemos

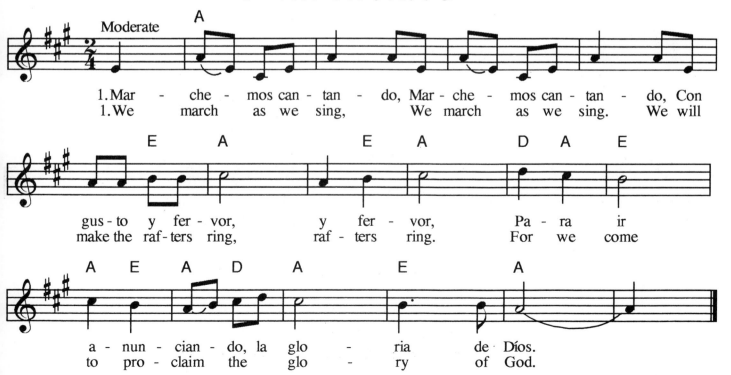

1. Mar - che - mos can - tan - do, Mar - che - mos can - tan - do, Con
1. We march as we sing, We march as we sing. We will

gus - to y fer - vor, y fer - vor, Pa - ra ir
make the raf - ters ring, raf - ters ring. For we come

a - nun - cian - do, la glo - ria de Díos.
to pro - claim the glo - ry of God.

Pedida de la Posada

Slowly

D   A 7

En   nom - bre   del   cie   -   lo,
In   the   name   of   hea   -   ven,

D

os   pi - do   po - sa   -   da.
give   us   a   place   of   shel   -   ter,

D7   G

Pu - es   no   pue - de an - dar   mi es -
for my   poor   wife can no   long   -   er   tra-vel this

A   D   A   D

po - sa a - ma   -   da.
hard rock- y   road.

2. Entren, santos peregrinos, reciben este rincón,
   No de_este pobre morada sino de mi corazón.

3. Dichosa esta casa que nos da posada
   Diós siempre le de su dicha sagrada.

2. Enter, my poor weary travellers, and take my house for your dwelling,
   Not just my poor house I offer to you, take, too, a place in my heart.

3. Blessed be this house which gives shelter to such poor weary travelers,
   Always God's grace will be yours as you showed mercy to them.

46

Canción de Piñata

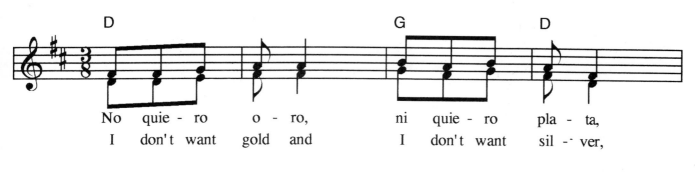

No quie - ro o - ro, ni quie - ro pla - ta,
I don't want gold and I don't want sil - ver,

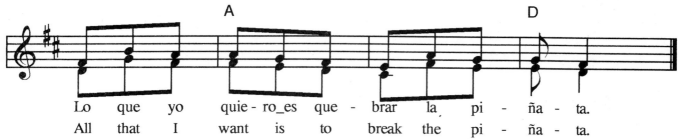

Lo que yo quie - ro_es que - brar la pi - ña - ta.
All that I want is to break the pi - ña - ta.

The piñata is an important part of childrens' celebrations. A paper maché container is molded into a fanciful shape, such as an animal or star, and covered all over with bright strips of tissue paper. An opening is left so that it can be filled with treats such as wrapped candy or nuts. The piñata is hung up securely and blindfolded children take turns trying to hit it with a large stick. As the piñata is broken the contents are scattered on the ground for the children to pick up.

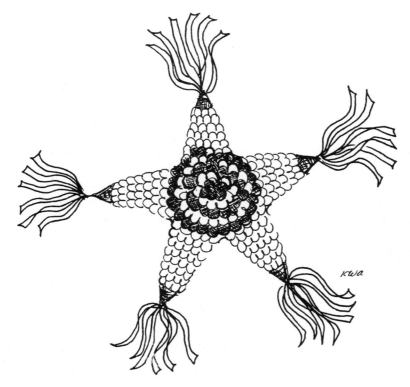

Las Posadas Play

CAST: Mary,
Joseph,
Innkeepers #1,#2 #3,
Boy who wants piñata,
2 children holding piñata,
Chorus of children

PROPS: Piñata (star shape or other) plus pole to hold it
Baseball bat or large stick
3 large child sized cardboard doors with windows
Colorful painted staff

COSTUMES: Girls: Mexican style colorful skirts and blouses
Boys: Tunic tops, shirts and slacks, rebozas, ponchos, colorful
embroidered belts and sombreros
Mary : A large blue stole to cover her head and body.
Joseph: Slacks, tunic or shirt, poncho and belt, decorated staff

STAGING: *Children proceed to stage to MARCHEMOS CANTANDO, which may
either be played on piano or sung. Inkeepers pick up their doors and stand
beside them, faces peering out of windows.*

*A chorus of children stands together at one side. Joseph, Mary and Boy
who wants piñata go from door to door. All sing PEDIDA DE LA POSADA.*

48

Joseph knocks on door #1 held by Innkeeper #1

JOSEPH: In the name of Heaven, I beg you for shelter.
           My beloved wife can walk no longer.

INNKEEPER #1: This is no inn. Continue on your way.
           I cannot open for you may be a thief.

Small group moves to door #2 held by Innkeeper #2. All sing PEDIDA DE LA POSADA aagain. Joseph knocks on door #2

JOSEPH: In the name of Heaven, I beg you for shelter.
           My beloved wife can walk no longer.

INNKEEPER #2: Go away now. Trouble me no more.
           If I lose my temper, you shall feel my stick.

Small group moves to door #3 held by Innkeeper #3. All sing PEDIDA DE LA POSADA. Joseph knocks on door #3

JOSEPH: In the name of Heaven, I beg you for shelter.
           My beloved wife can walk no longer.

INNKEEPER #3: Enter, holy travelers, and accept this place
           not only in this poor dwelling but in my heart.

MARY: Blessed is this house which gives us shelter.
           God will give you His blessed grace always.

Innkeeper #3 "opens" door. Piñata is brought out by 2 children from backstage. It is suspended on a pole carried on their shoulders. Boy who wants piñata moves forward.

BOY: I don't want gold. I don't want silver.
           All that I want is to break the pinata!

All sing CANCION DE PIÑATA. Children holding piñata and boy who wants piñata lead off stage, followed by Mary and Joseph and Chorus of Children. At this point the piñata may be broken if desired.

HISPANIC SINGING GAMES

Life on the big ranchos was family oriented and large families were the rule rather than the exception. Early sources speak of the sound of children's laughter ringing throughout the haciendas.

Games, particularly singing games, were an important part of the lives of these children. Almost without exception, the games came over from the Old World with the early Spanish settlers. Many have their counterparts in other cultures throughout Europe and the British Isles.

Al Citrón

This is an old Spanish game song based on passing an object to the beat of the music. There is no translation as nonsense words are used.

Game Instructions: Children are seated in a circle on the ground. Each child has a small stick (rhythm stick or ruler), which is passed to the right. On the *al ci* the stick is picked up and on the *tron* it is passed to the neighbor on the right. This continues around the circle until the words *triki triki tron,* when the stick is held and tapped right and left and then passed on the final word *tron.* The game is simplified if left hands are held behind backs. A trial run without sticks, hands going through the motions on the words "pick up - pass" is highly recommended

El Florón

El Florón (The Big Flower) is a traditional children's game that settlers brought from Spain to Mexico and from Mexico to California. This guessing game involves some skill at sleight of hand.

El flo - rón an-da_en las ma - nos, en las ma - nos, y_en las
Hand to hand the flow - er tra - vels, flow-er tra - vels. Now in

man-os lo_han de_ha-llar. A - di - vi - nen quien lo tie - ne,
some one's hand it lies. You must guess the one who has it,

quien lo tie - ne o se que - da de plan- tón.
one who has it, and you on - ly get three tries.

Game Instructions: Before the game begins, a guesser is chosen who stands outside the circle and watches closely as the game proceeds. Children form a circle and extend their cupped hands. While they sing the song, one child passes the *florón* (a flower-like object, small enough to be concealed within the hands). The child pretends to give it to each member of the circle, but in reality secretly slips it to only one child. After completing the circle, the passer returns to his or her place and the guesser makes the three guesses to discover who holds the *florón*.

51

El Sombrero Blanco

This song, together with its dance, is referred to in almost every early source for the Rancho period. The colors white and blue refer to the white or blue bands worn on sombreros to identify rival political factions of the time. Melody is the lower of the two parts.

El Sombrero Blanco

Chorus:
¿Quieres que te ponga mi sombrero blanco?
¿Quieres que te ponga mi sombrero azul?
¿Quieres que te siente, mi vida, en un trono?
Para que te cante el tu run tun, tur un tun,
   tu-run tun, tun.

1. Si quieres que yo te quiera,
   Manda_enladrillar el mar
   Y despues de_enladrillado
   Soy tuyo y puedes mandar.

2. Si quieres que yo te quiera
   Ha de ser con condición,
   Que lo tuyo_ha de ser mío
   Y la mío tuyo no.

Chorus:
Will you let me place on your head my sombrero?
Will you let me place there my sombrero blue?
Will you let me seat you, my dear, on a throne?
So that I may sing to you, tu run tun, tu run tun,
   tu run tun, tun.

1. If you should wish that I might love you
   You should order the sea paved with stone
   And when this is done then call me,
   My heart will be yours alone!

2. If you should wish that I might love you
   There is just one thing you must do.
   Give to me all your possessions,
   But I will give nothing to you.

Dance Instructions

A number of couples can perform this dance, either in line or circle formation. The boy has his hands behind his back. The girl holds her skirts. Before the music begins, the dancers bow to one another.

Section A, Measures 1-8: Dancers circle each other with quick waltz steps, bending from the waist, side to side to the music. On the word *azul* the dancers face one another. The girl curtsies and the boy places his sombrero on her head.

Measures 9-19: Dancers face one another, taking three waltz steps forward and three back, then three waltz steps forward and bow on *tun* (measure 18).

Section B, Measures 20-28: Boy joins his right hand with partner's left and the girl circles him counterclockwise. Boy keeps left hand behind back. Girl holds skirt with right hand.

Measures 29-36: Couple switches hands and girl circles boy clockwise. If using chorus and second verse, dance begins again. Dancers bow to one another at end of dance.

El Borrego

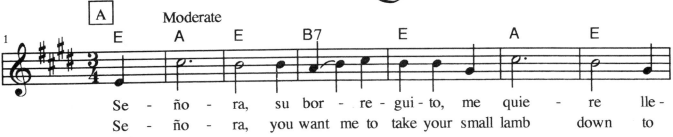

El Borrego
Dance Instructions

In the early Rancho days, any entertainment in which dancing was a major event was called a *fandango*. At a typical *fandango* one of the first dances was reserved for the children. *El Borrego* (The Lamb) was a popular children's dance of the time. The steps imitate a humorous mock battle similar to a bull fight.

This is a game song danced by partners. The two dancers stand opposite one another about five feet apart. Each carries a red handkerchief.

Section A, Measures 1-16: During the singing of the verse, the two dancers pantomime the words using walking steps, little runs, etc.

Section B: When the chorus is sung, the dancers shake their kerchiefs from side to side in a teasing manner, using little waltz steps. When the word *borreguito* is used, the boy prepares to attack. He lowers his head, puts his hands behind his back and on the first *tope* he butts his head forward, going under the kerchief held by the girl as both dancers exchange places. On the second *tope que tope* the action is repeated.

55

Víbora de la Mar

This game is the Hispanic version of London Bridge.

Ví - bo-ra, Ví - bo-ra de la mar, por a - quí pue - den pa - sar.
Sea ser - pent, sea ser - pent from the sea, You must fol-low, fol-low me;

Por a - quí yo pa - sa - ré y_un-a ni - ña de - jar - é.
Un-der this arch - way we must glide, and we'll leave a girl in - side.

U - na ni - ña cual se - rá? La de_a-de - lan-te_o la de_a - trás?
One lit-tle girl, who can she be? One a - head or back of me?

La de_ade-lan - te cor - re mu-cho, y la de_a trás se que - da - rá.
That one a-head, how she runs a-way, So the last one has to stay.

Game instructions: Two children are chosen to form the arch of a bridge (in large groups, two or three arches can be formed). The arch people each select one of two similar items such as red/green, apple/pear. The group sings and steps to the beat in circle formation, passing under the arch. On the last words of the song, the "arch" captures the one who is passing under . The arch people take the captured child aside and whisper the choices. After making the choice, the child stands behind that person and the game resumes. At the end of the game, there is a tug of war between the two sides.

RUSSIAN MUSIC AT FORT ROSS

FORT ROSS

A diagram showing the buildings within the compound at Fort Ross based on journals, letters, drawings and maps of the period. The stockade had the same characteristics as a number of Russian fortresses built in Siberia, the northern Pacific islands and Alaska. Although the purpose of the settlement was for otter hunting, trade and agriculture, the Russians felt the need to fortify. They felt surrounded by potentially hostile forces as Spain, Mexico, England, France and the United States all opposed the Russian presence in California.

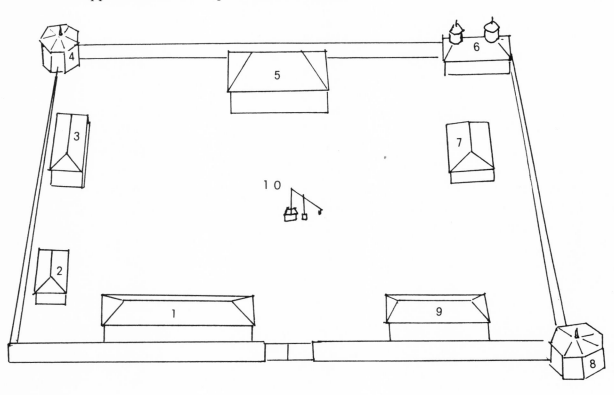

1. Official's barracks: provided company officials and visitors with rooms.
2. Rotchev House: built in 1836, served as Commandant's house until 1841.
3. Fur Barn: storage for furs and agricultural produce.
4. North Blockhouse: fitted out with muskets and cannon, protected the northern stockade walls.
5. Kuskov House: served as Commandant's house until 1836. Living quarters were upstairs while the lower level contained the storeroom and armory.
6. Chapel: built in 1824. First Russian Orthodox church in North America outside of Alaska.
7. Employee's Barracks: provided living quarters for unmarried men. Families lived outside the stockade walls in individual houses.
8. South Blockhouse: protected southern stockade walls.
9. Kitchen: originally a warehouse. Later converted into a common kitchen.
10. Well: although water outside the stockade was plentiful, the compound well offered security in case of attack.

RUSSIAN MUSIC AT FORT ROSS

The view of Fort Ross, dominating the headland, is one of the most dramatic sights along the northern California coast. Now a State Historic Park, it stands as a living reminder of Russia's attempt to establish a foothold in the New World.

In 1805 Count Nikolai Resanov, the Czar's chamberlain, traveled from Moscow to inspect the Alaskan fur posts of the Russian-American Company. He found a desperate shortage of food, especially the fruits and vegetables needed to ward off scurvy. Resanov's solution was to explore the possibility of establishing a base in California to furnish food for the Alaskan outposts.

Ivan Kuskov, agent for the Russia-America Company, was sent to California in the company of Aleut seal hunters, to scout for a suitable site. He settled on an area on the Sonoma coast near the mouth of the Russian River. Construction was completed in 1812 and the settlement was called Rossiya, an ancient term for Russia. Today, it is known as Fort Ross.

The buildings consisted of a commandant's house, barracks, quarters for the Russian employees, and various storehouses and lesser buildings. A chapel was added in 1824. All of these structures were placed within a stockade and guarded by two blockhouses with mounted cannon.

Outside the stockade walls were the dwellings of the Aleuts and Kashaya Pomo people. There were very few women among the Russian settlers, and both Russians and Aleuts married Kashaya women. In the end the population at the Fort became inextricably mixed.

The land around Fort Ross itself was limited and not very fertile. Despite continued efforts at farming, sea-otter hunting, and a certain amount of trading with the Californios, the colony never prospered. In 1841, John A. Sutter purchased the livestock and other movable property at the fort and the last vestiges of the Czar's frontier in California finally disappeared.

During their relatively brief presence on the northern California coast, the Russians were strangers in a strange land. They held on to as many of the traditions and customs of their homeland as they possibly could. The songs they brought with them were drawn from the rich and beautiful folk heritage of "Mother Russia."

Kalinka

This old Russian song may have been danced and sung on social occasions at Fort Ross such as the birthday celebration for Elena Rotcheva, wife of the last Russian Commandant. In true Slavic tradition, the tempo of the chorus begins slowly and gradually accelerates.

Kalinka
Dance Instructions

Dancers stand side by side, facing in opposite directions. Each reaches across front of partner and places hand on partner's waist. The girl carries a scarf in her raised free hand. The boy keeps his free hand raised also. As the tempo of the chorus begins slowly and becomes faster and faster, the dancers twirl in time to the music.

Russian Pronunciation Guide

a as in bar   o as in bore
e as in bed   u as in blue
i as in bid or bead   ay as in buy
y as in bill (dull i)   ey as in reign

kh is a guttural aspirant as in the Scottish loch
zh as in the French jamais

The apostrophe after a consonant denotes a softening
(e.g. the l in tol'ko is pronounced as in "well yes" or the
t in byt' as in "but yes.")

Beryozonka

Beryozonka (The Birch Tree) is one of Russia's oldest and most beloved folk songs and is a song which the Russian settlers at Fort Ross would have known and sung. Tchaikovsky used the melody, with some alterations, in the Finale of his Fourth Symphony. This song may be sung as a three part canon (round).

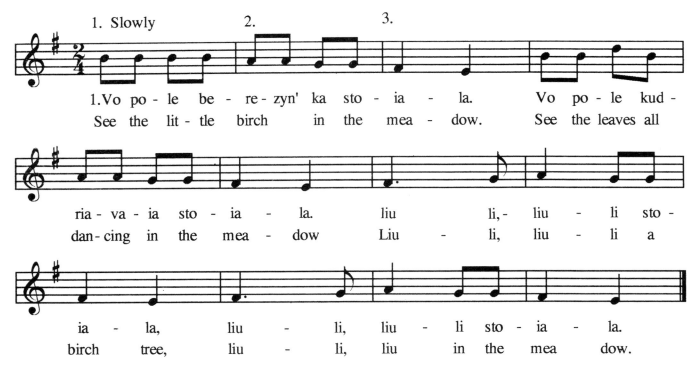

1. Vo po - le be - re - zyn' ka sto - ia - la. Vo po - le kud -
See the lit - tle birch in the mea - dow. See the leaves all

ria - va - ia sto - ia - la. liu li, - liu - li sto -
dan - cing in the mea - dow Liu - li, liu - li a

ia - la, liu - li, liu - li sto - ia - la.
birch tree, liu - li, liu in the mea dow.

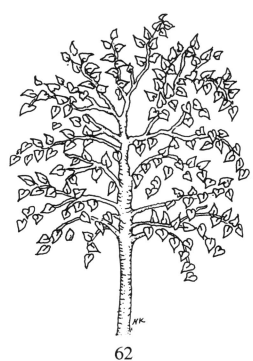

MEXICAN AMERICAN WAR SONGS

TERRITORY GAINED FROM MEXICO

1848

Columbia River

OREGON TERRITORY

UNITED STATES

MEXICAN CESSION
(Treaty of Guadalupe Hidalgo)

Great Salt Lake

UNORGANIZED TERRITORY

Colorado River

TEXAS

N
W E
S

MEXICO

Rio Grande

Pacific Ocean

MEXICAN AMERICAN
WAR SONGS

The California state flag with its brown grizzly bear on a field of white is a symbol of the conflict that marked the transition from California as a province of the Mexican Republic to California as a part of the Untied States.

The Mexican-American war was fought between the U. S. and Mexico over territorial disagreements that had been accumulating for two decades. The larger conflict took place in Mexico itself with Mexican troops led by General Antonio Lopez de Santa Anna and U.S. troops led by General Zachary Taylor.

The war reached California in June, 1846, when a group of American settlers revolted against the Mexican Government. This rebellion became known as the Bear Flag Revolt because of the portrayal of a grizzly bear on the settlers' flag. In July, U.S. naval forces captured Monterey and occupied the San Francisco area. In December, General Stephen Kearny led his troops in the bloody battle of San Pasqual near San Diego. In January, 1847, Kearny of the U.S. Army and Stockton of the U.S. Navy won the battle of San Gabriel near Los Angeles. With this victory, the American conquest of California was complete.

The war came to an end with the Americans and Mexicans signing the Treaty of Guadalupe Hidalgo in 1848. The terms of the treaty ceded to the U. S. the regions of California, Nevada and Utah, most of Arizona and New Mexico, and parts of Colorado and Wyoming. The United States paid Mexico $15 million for this land. California became the thirty-first state on September 9, 1850.

Although wars, with their often murky causes, are fought between different nations and in different times, the kinds of songs sung by soldiers remain pretty much the same. They sing about home and sweethearts, fatalism in the face of death, heroes and feats of valor, drinking and carousing , and humorous grousing about army life in general. The songs of the soldiers, both Mexican and American, who drank and sang in the taverns and cantinas and who fought and died on the battlefields of Mexico and California are no different.

Green Grow the Laurels

This song was so widely sung by the American soldiers at the time of the Mexican-American War that the Mexicans identified them by the first two words of the song "green grow" (*gringo*).

1. Green grow the lau - rels, all spark - ling with dew. I'm
lone - ly my dar - ling since part - ing from you, But
by the next meet - ing I hope to prove true, And
change the green lau - rel for the red, white and blue.

2. I once had a sweetheart but now I have none
   Since she's gone and left me, I care not for one,
   Since she's gone and left me, contented I'll be,
   For she loves another one better than me.

3. I passed my love's window both early and late,
   The look that she gave me would make your heart ache.
   O the look that she gave me was painful to see,
   For she loves another one better than me.

4. I wrote my love letters in red rosy lines,
   She wrote me an answer all twisted in twines,
   Saying "Keep your love letters and I will keep mine,
   Just you write to your love and I'll write to mine."

Santy Anno

One of the most popular of all capstan shanties carries the name of the Mexican general, Antonio Lopez de Santa Anna, who was defeated by General Zachary Taylor at the battle of Molina del Rey in the Mexican-American War. Santa Anna was renowned as both a soldier and political leader in the earliest days of the Mexican Republic. General Taylor went on to become president of the United States.

2. She's a fast clipper ship and a bully good crew,
   A down east Yankee for her captain, too.

3. There's plenty of gold so I've been told,
   There's plenty of gold so I've been told.

4. Back in the days of Forty-nine,
   Those were the days of the good old times.

5. When Zacharias Taylor gained the day,
   He made poor Santy run away.

6. General Scott and Taylor, too,
   Made poor Santy meet his Waterloo.

7. Santy Anno was a good old man,
   Till he got into war with your Uncle Sam.

8. When I leave this ship I will settle down,
   And marry a girl named Sally Brown.

El Tecolote

El Tecolote is a soldier's song from New Mexico, popular among Santa Anna's troops. *Tecolote* is an Aztec word for owl.

Lyrics under the music:

¿ Te - co - lo - te, de don - de vie - nes? ¿ Te - co -
Te - co - lo - te, where do you come from? Te - co -

lo - te, de don - de vie - nes? Del pue - blo de Co - lo -
lo - te, where do you come from? From the town of Co - lo -

ri - do, del Pue - blo de Co - lo - ri - do, ay!
ri - do From the town of Co - lo - ri - do. Ay!

Chorus

Pá - ja - ro, cu - cu, cu, Pá - ja - ro, cu - cu,
Lit tle bird, cu, cu, cu, Lit - tle bird, cu, cu,

cu. Po - bre - ci - to a - ni - ma - li - to, tie - ne
cu, Poor little owl, he's cry - ing with hun - ger, Poor little

ham - bre_el te - co - lo - ti - to, ay!
owl, he's cry - ing with hun - ger, Ay!

2. Vengo de hacer ejercicio (2X)
En las tropas de Santa Anna
En las tropas de Santa Anna, Ay!

2. I've been keeping very fit, sir (2X)
With the troops of Santa Anna,
With the troops of Santa Anna, Ay!

Clarín de Campaña

A favorite with Santa Anna's troops, Clarín de Campaña (The Trumpet of Battle) expresses a theme typical of many soldiers' songs: "Eat, drink and be merry, for tomorrow we die."

Mien tras ten-gan li-cor las bo - te-llas, ha-ga-mos con
While there's wine in the bot-tle for - get woe and wor - ry, For-

e - llas mas dul-ce_el vi - vir. Mien - tras
get ev - ery troub - le and sigh. While there's

Re - cor - dan-do que tal vez ma - ña - na cla - rín de com-
For to - mor-row the can-nons may thun - der, the trum - pet of

pa - ña nos lla-me_a mo - rir. Re - cor rir. -
bat - tle may call us to die. For to die. -

2. Mientras tengan perfume las flores,
   Olviden dolores y vengan a_amar (2X)
   Recordando que tal vez mañana,
   Clarín de campaña nos llame_a pelear. (2X)

2. While the flowers and their perfume enchant us,
   Forget all our sorrows. There's only tonight. (2X)
   For tomorrow the cannons may thunder
   The trumpet of battle may call us to fight. (2X)

WESTWARD SEA ROUTES

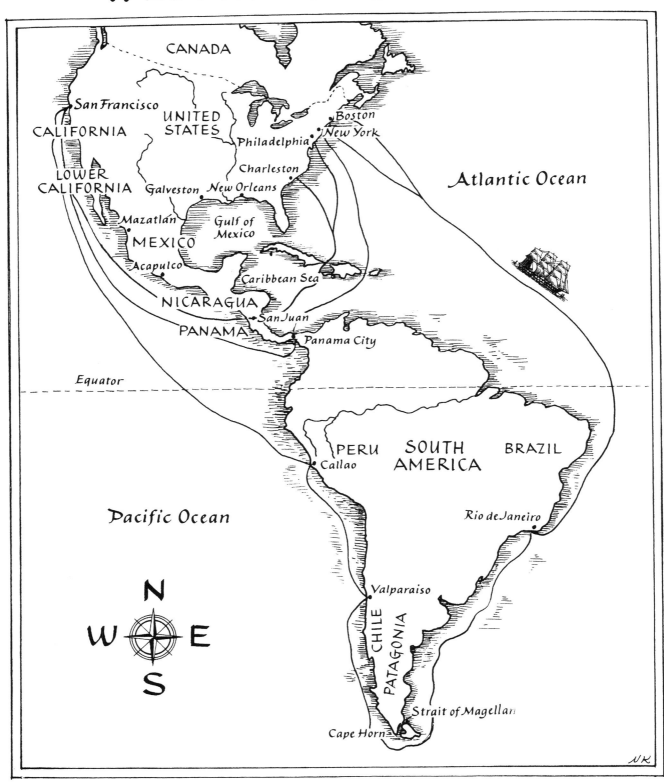

CANADA

San Francisco
CALIFORNIA

UNITED STATES

Boston
New York
Philadelphia

Charleston

Atlantic Ocean

LOWER CALIFORNIA

Galveston
New Orleans

Mazatlán

Gulf of Mexico

MEXICO

Acapulco

Caribbean Sea

NICARAGUA

San Juan

PANAMA

Panama City

Equator

PERU

SOUTH AMERICA

BRAZIL

Callao

Pacific Ocean

Rio de Janeiro

Valparaiso

CHILE

PATAGONIA

Strait of Magellan

Cape Horn

N
W   E
S

NK

SHANTIES
OF THE
SAILING
SHIPS

SHANTIES OF THE SAILING SHIPS

California's openness to the great Pacific has been a crucial factor affecting her historical destiny. Along her 840 mile coastline are two great natural harbors, San Francisco and San Diego. Songs of seafarers have been heard in California since the days of the early explorers and were at their peak during the Golden Age of Sail (1820-1860).

Sea commerce in California, which started with the hide trade, truly opened up in the middle of the 1800's with the discovery of gold. An ever increasing number of ships sailed into San Francisco Bay bringing both fortune seekers and settlers to the "Golden Land." Merchant vessels brought supplies to service this booming population. Sperm whaling was also a major industry during the nineteenth century. Although it was chiefly based in the New England seaports, much whaling took place in the Pacific with San Francisco as its major whaling port.

The main sea route to California involved coming around Cape Horn and up the coasts of South America and Mexico to San Francisco. The journey around the Horn was a fearful one with its sixty foot waves, its savage unremitting winds, hail, sleet, lightning and massive icebergs. Many ships were lost with all hands.

The ships which brought gold-seekers, emigrants and supplies were full-rigged deep-water vessels which required crews of twenty to fifty men. The back-breaking work of hauling tons of yards and canvas up the masts, furling and bracing sail, and heaving on the capstan bars or pump handles was done totally with human labor. The singing of worksongs (sea shanties) helped to put extra energy into this work. It was said that a good shanty was worth ten extra men.

There were appropriate shanties for every big job aboard ship and the crew member designated to lead them was called a "shanty man." He chose a good shanty for the job at hand and sang the solo parts as the crew joined in on the refrains and chorus. Many of the verses he sang were interchangeable from one shanty to another. Others he improvised, attempting to amuse the crew with sly comments about life aboard ship or bawdy references to good times in the ports.

SHANTY TYPES

Teamwork aboard ship required either short or long pulls or pushes. For jobs requiring only a few short powerful pulls, the SHORT HAUL shanty was used. The pull usually came on one or two words in the chorus.

The HALYARD shanty was used to haul up yards (wooden crossbeams) to which sails were attached. The crew hauled only on the chorus which gave the men a chance to rest for a few seconds before the next strong pull on the ropes.

Windlass and bilge-pumping work was stationary, requiring an up and down motion with the hands and arms. PUMPING and WINDLASS shanties helped to coordinate this motion.

The capstan (pronounced caps'n) was a barrel shaped apparatus around which a cable was wrapped. Bars were inserted into the top section and, as the men pushed on the bars, the cable wound around and lifted whatever was attached (anchor, cargo, etc.) As the work involved pushing around in a circle at a steady pace, a march-like cadence distinguished the CAPSTAN shanty.

Unlike sea shanties, which were work songs, FORECASTLE songs (pronounced foc'sle) were songs of leisure, sung when a hard days work was finally completed. Joanna Colcord, in her book *Songs of the American Sailormen*, wrote:

> When the day's work was over, supper eaten and the mess kits put away and pipes or cheeks, as the case might be, filled with strong plug tobacco, came the sailor's time of leisure. During the "dog watch" in the early evening, both watches were on deck, gathered about the main hatch in pleasant weather or stowed away in sheltered spots when it was inclement. Singing, dancing and yarn spinning were the order of the day; cherished instruments were brought out, perhaps a squeaky old accordian, beloved of the sailor and hated, for some unknown reason, by every master mariner I ever knew.

Haul Away, Joe

Short Haul Shanty

In this humorous shanty, the forceful pull on the ropes takes place on the word "Joe."

1. When I was a lit - tle lad and so my mo - ther told me,

'Way, haul a way, we'll haul a - way Joe! That

if I did - n't kiss the girls my lips would grow all mol - dy,

'Way, haul a way, we'll haul a - way Joe!

2. King Louis was the King of France before the Revolution,
   But then he got his head cut off which spoiled his constitution.

3. Once I was in Ireland a-diggin' turf and praties,*
   But now I'm on a Yankee ship a-haulin' sheets and braces.

4. Way, haul away, we'll haul for better weather,
   Way, haul away, we'll hang and haul together.

* Praties = Potatoes

A Long Time Ago

Halyard Shanty

This popular halyard shanty was sung on both British and American ships. The third verse, "Her masts was silver; her yards was gold," describes the white painted masts and varnished yards on American ships.

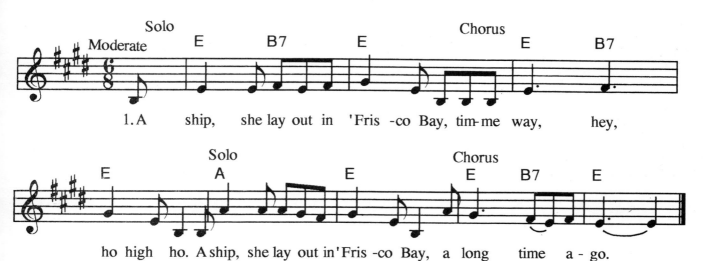

1. A ship, she lay out in 'Fris-co Bay, tim-me way, hey, ho high ho. A ship, she lay out in 'Fris-co Bay, a long time a-go.

2. This smart Yankee packet lay out in the bay,
   A-waiting a wind for to get under way.

3. Her masts was silver; her yards was gold.
   Her masts was silver; her yards was gold.

4. We sailed out of Frisco in a full rigged ship.
   We sailed out of Frisco in a full rigged ship.

5. We was bound for New York with a cargo o' gold,
   Bound South 'round the Horn through the ice and the cold.

6. With all her poor sailors so weak an' so sad,
   They'd drunk all their lime juice; no more could be had.

John Kanaka

Halyard Shanty

Richard Henry Dana, in his book <u>Two Years Before the Mast</u>, refers to the singing of work songs by the Kanaka (Hawaiian) crews of ships loading hides on the California coast. The chorus of this song is thought to be of Polynesian origin.

2. I thought I heard the bosun say
   "We'll work tomorrer, but no work today."

3. We're bound away for Frisco Bay,
   We're bound away at the break of day.

4. A Yankee ship with a Yankee crew,
   We're the buckos for to push her through.

5. Oh haul away, oh haul away,
   Oh, haul away and make your pay.

76

John Kanaka
Dance Instructions

A. Partners are chosen. They join hands and twirl (or do-si-do) to the first line of the song

B. On line two, partners perform the following actions:
      "John" - each partner stamps right foot
      "naka, naka" - knock knees together two times
      "Tu" - Slap own thighs
      "Lai" - Clap own hands
      "Ay" - partners touch palms together

On line 3 repeat part A.

On line 4 repeat part B.

C. On line 5 dancers must find **new** partners in time to repeat Part B on line 6.

Reuben Ranzo

Halyard Shanty

Reuben Ranzo was one of the few songs sung on board whaling ships. The melody comes from an old Sicilian fisherman's song. Many ships couldn't find enough experienced sailors for their long sea voyages. In this song the crew makes fun of the inexperienced sailor -- Reuben Ranzo.

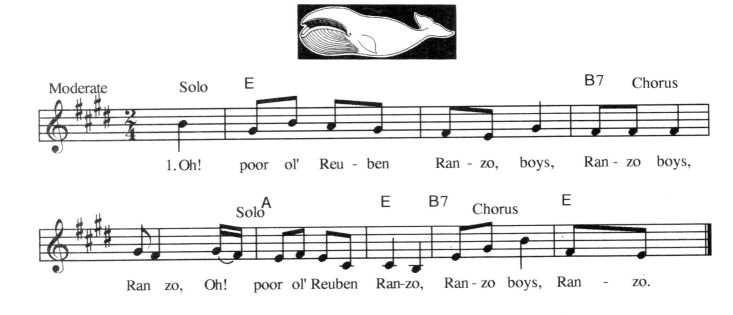

2. Oh, Ranzo was no sailor, boys,
   He was a New York tailor.

3. Though Ranzo was no sailor, boys,
   He shipped aboard a whaler.

4. Oh, Ranzo couldn't steer 'er, boys,
   Did you ever hear anything queerer?

5. The mate he was a dandy, boys,
   Far too fond of brandy.

6. They said he was a lubber, boys,
   And made him eat whale blubber.

7. He washed once in a fortnight, boys,
   He said it was his birthright.

8. They gave him lashes thirty, boys,
   Because he was so dirty.

9. The Cap'n gave him thirty, boys,
   His daughter begged for mercy.

10. She gave him cake and water, boys,
    And a bit more than she oughter.

11. She taught him navigation, boys,
    And gave him eddication.

12. Oh, Ranzo now is skipper, boys,
    Of a Yankee whaler.

13. He married the Old Man's daughter, boys,
    And still sails on blue water.

Goodbye. Fare Ye Well

Windlass Shanty

An early type of windlass shanty was a four-liner with two line solos and refrains. "Goodbye, Fare-ye-well," one of the most beloved homeward bound shanties, was traditionally sung aboad departing ships. Men from other ships moored in the harbor added their voices to swell the chorus.

1. Oh, don't you hear the Old Man say? Good bye, fare-ye-well, Good bye, fare-ye-well. Oh, don't you hear the Old Man say? Hoo-rah, me boys, we're home-ward bound!

2. We're homeward bound to the gals o' the town,
   Stamp up, me bullies, and heave it around.

3. We're homeward bound and the anchor's a-weigh,
   The gals will be waiting to spend all our pay.

4. We'll spend all our money in one week ashore,
   And then pack our bags and go sailing once more.

79

Row. Bullies Row

Capstan Shanty

This song, of Irish origin, was mentioned by Richard Henry Dana in his book <u>Cruise Off California</u> in the 1830's and was sung aboard hide carriers at that time.

2. The clipper ship, Comet, lies out in the bay,
   A-waiting a fair wind to get under way,
   The sailors on board are so sick and so sore,
   For their liquor's all gone and they can't get no more.

3. That night off Cape Horn, I won't soon forget,
   It gives me the horrors to think of it yet,
   We were diving bows under and all of us wet,
   A-making twelve knots with the skysails all set.

4. Here's to our Captain, where'er he may be,
   He's a friend to the sailor on land or on sea,
   But as to the first mate, that dirty old brute,
   I hope when he dies straight below he will shoot.

Leave Her Johnny

Capstan Shanty

This was traditionally sung at the end of a voyage before sailors went ashore to collect their pay. It was a means of airing grievances against the ship's officers, the food, and the owners.

Oh the times was hard and the wa- ges low. Leave her, John-ny, leave her. But now once more a-shore we'll go, for it's time for us to leave her. Leave her, John - ny, leave her. Oh, leave her, John - ny, leave her. We'll pack our bags and go be - low for it's time for us to leave her.

2. The winds was foul, all work, no pay,
   From Liverpool docks to Frisco Bay.

3. We was made to pump all night and day,
   And we, half dead, had beggar-all to say.

4. Mahogany beef and weevils in our bread,
   Sometimes we wished that cook was dead.

5. The sails is furled and our work is done,
   And now ashore we'll have our bit of fun.

81

Sacramento

Capstan Shanty

"Sacramento" recounts in seamen's words the long journey around Cape Horn to the California gold fields. It resembles Stephen Foster's Camptown Races. Foster did not copyright Camptown Races until 1850 and there are records of seamen singing "Sacramento" in 1849. One can only guess which song came first.

Oh, a - round Cape Horn we are bound for to go, to me hoo - dah, to me

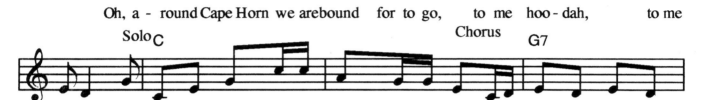

hoo dah, A - round Cape Horn through the sleet and the snow, to me hoo - dah, hoo - dah

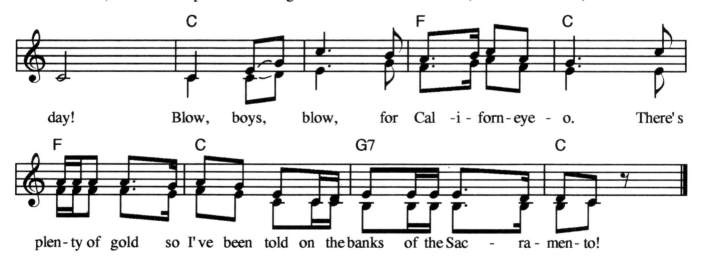

day! Blow, boys, blow, for Cal -i - forn - eye - o. There's

plen - ty of gold so I've been told on the banks of the Sac - ra - men - to!

2. Oh, around Cape Horn in the month of May,
   Around Cape Horn is a bloody long way.

3. Oh around Cape Horn with a main sail set,
   Around Cape Stiff and we're all wringing wet.

4. To the Sacramento we're bound away,
   For there the gold's more bright than day.

5. Round the Horn and up to the line,
   We're the buckos for to make her shine.

6. Breast your bars and bend your backs,
   Heave and make your spare ribs crack.

7. Ninety days to Frisco Bay,
   Ninety days for to make our pay.

8. Those Spanish girls ain't got no combs,
   They comb their hair with tunny-fish bones.

9. Oh, those were the days of the good old times,
   Back in the days of the Forty-nine.

Away, Rio

Capstan Shanty

Rio Grande do Sul, on the east coast of Brazil, was one of the seamen's favorite ports. In this
popular outward bound song, Rio is pronounced Rye-o.

2. Our good ships a-sailing out over the bar,
   We've pointed her bow to the Southern Star.

3. Oh man the good capstan and run it around,
   We'll heave in the sugar and then homeward bound.

4. Heave with a will and heave long and strong,
   Sing the good chorus for 'tis a good song.

The Leaving of Liverpool

Foc'sle Shanty

The Yankee clipper ship *Davy Crockett,* was launched in 1853 in Mystic, Connecticut.
The *Crockett* was under the command of Captain John Burgess from 1863 until he
was lost overboard 11 years later. He regularly sailed back and forth from Liverpool, England,
to California. The ship's figurehead may be found in the San Francisco Maritime Museum.

Fare thee well to Prin - ce's land - ing stage, Ri-ver Mer - sey, fare thee
well. I'm off for Cal - i - forn - i-ay, a place I know right
well. So fare thee well, my own true love, when
I re-turn u - ni-ted we shall be, It's not the leav - ing of Li - ver - pool that
grieves me but my dar - ling when I think of thee.

2. Now I'm off to Cali-forni-ay, by way of cruel Cape Horn,
   And I'll send to you a letter, love, when again I am homeward bound.

3. I have shipped aboard a Yankee clipper ship, *Davy Crockett* is her name,
   And Burgess is the captain of her and they say she's a floating hell.

4. The tug is waiting at the old pierhead, to take us down the stream;
   Our sails are loosed and our anchor secure, so I'll bid you good-bye once more.

THE WAY WEST:

SONGS
OF THE
OVERLAND
EMIGRANTS

OVERLAND ROUTES WESTWARD

Oregon Trail ------
California Trail --.--.--
Sante Fe Trail ....
Old Spanish Trail -..-..-

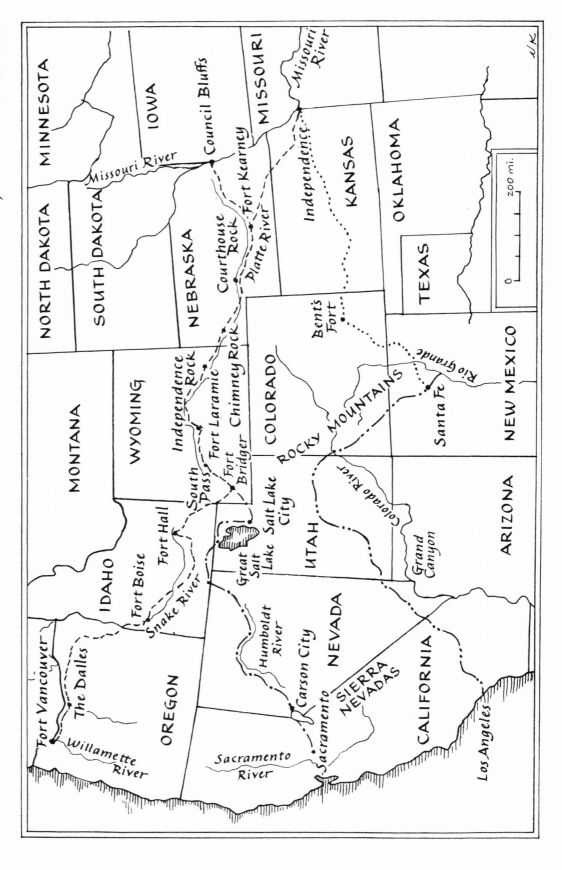

86

THE WAY WEST:
SONGS OF THE OVERLAND EMIGRANTS

Songs of the overland travelers to California from the East often make light of ordeals and turn hardships into rough jokes. Behind the humor, however, are stories of heroic perseverance and high adventure.

In the early 1840's, sailors, scouts and trappers returned East with reports of the fabled land of California, a land of perennial spring and boundless fertility. A small number of emigrants risked the grueling overland route, using trails established by fur traders and mountain men. After gold was discovered in 1849, the trickle of emigrants became a flood.

Of the four principal routes, the most popular was the 2,100 mile California-Oregon Trail. From the Missouri frontier this trail followed the Platte River and crossed the Rocky Mountains to Fort Bridger in what is now Wyoming. There the California Trail branched off to Salt Lake and continued along the Humboldt and Truckee Rivers to Sacramento.

Emigrants gathered in the small towns of western Missouri and Iowa such as St. Joseph, Independence and Council Bluffs, to form their wagon trains. While they waited for spring grasses to provide food for the animals, the emigrant families organized their supplies and got to know one another. Food provisions were limited to staples that would not spoil. Once the emigrants were on the trail, hunting and fishing supplemented the diet. Many families brought along a cow for milk.

Wagon trains usually started out in May, having only four to five months to reach and cross the Sierra before snow blocked the passes. Most parties consisted of fifteen to thirty wagons and had a leader and scouts who knew the trail. Teams of mules or oxen pulled wagons that were covered with canvas to form a tent-like enclosure. As they moved out across the prairie they looked like ships at sea and were dubbed "Prairie Schooners." Many wagons had slogans like "California or Bust," or "Meet You at Sutter's Fort," painted on their sides. To make it in time to avoid the snow, they had to average between fourteen and sixteen miles a day, allowing for storms, breakdowns, and difficult ferry crossings on makeshift rafts.

A day on the trail began at dawn. Women built fires and cooked breakfast while the men hitched up the teams. The travelers stopped before noon and rested several hours before the long, hard afternoon trek began. Before sundown, the wagons were pulled into a rough circle and teams unhitched. One traveler (G. W. Thissell) wrote in his notebook:

> The most pleasant part of the trip was around the campfire. Supper over, dishes and pots out of the way, we would gather around the campfire and relate scenes of the day and spin long yarns. Some played the violin, others the accordion. A few would play cards, while the young men would sing their favorite California songs.

By the time they reached the western deserts and mountains the weary travelers still had the second half of their journey to face. They had been on the trail for about three months and accidents, illness, the threat of Indian attacks and exposure to the elements had taken their toll. Rude crosses along the trail marked the last resting places of loved ones and friends. After enduring all these hardships travelers still had to face the desert heat and cold. Many of the animals died or were killed for food. When the emigrants reached the Carson River in Nevada, they felt the worst was over even though they still had the Sierra Nevada to cross.

Of the 20,000 people who started along the California Trail in 1849, about 750 died along the way. Many arrived in California so sick and worn out that they never recovered. Half of the animals and wagons never made it.

The record of the way west is found in the diaries and memoirs of those who survived the ordeal. The long, courageous journey across plains, rivers, deserts and mountains was one of the great adventures of our country.

On the Road to Californey

Singing helped travelers pass the time during the long journey west. This humorous song is a
California version of the old song Kansas Boys.

Come all girls, pay at-ten-tion to my voice, don't you fall in love with the
Kan-sas boys, for if you do your for-tune it will be:
Hoe cakes, ho-mi-ny and sas-sa-fras tea. On the road to
Ca-li-for-ney, it was a hard and te-di-ous jour-ney.
Far a-cross the Rock-y Mountains, crys-tal springs and flow-ing foun-tains.

2. When they go to meeting, the clothes they wear,
   An old brown coat all fixed and bare.
   An old white hat small rimmed and crowned,
   A pair of cotton socks that they wore the year 'round.

3. Some live in a cabin with a huge log wall,
   And nary a window in it at all,
   A sandstone chimney and a punch board floor,
   A clap board roof and a button hole door.

Sweet Betsy from Pike

Missouri, the "Gateway to the West," was the departure point for many of the California emigrants. Pike County, Missouri, in the northeastern section of the state, is mentioned in several songs including "Sweet Betsy from Pike" which is one of the best known songs of the Westward Movement.

Did you ev - er hear tell of sweet Bet - sy from Pike, who crossed the wide prai - ries with her lov - er Ike, with two yoke of cat - tle and one spot - ted hog, a tall Shang - hai roost - er and an old yal - ler dog. Hoo dle dang fol di dye - do, hoo dle dang fol - di day. Hoo dle dang fol - di dye - do, hoo dle dang fol - di day.

Sweet Betsy from Pike

1. Did you ever hear tell of Sweet Betsy from Pike,
   Who crossed the wide prairies with her lover, Ike,
   With two yoke of cattle and one spotted hog,
   A tall Shanghai rooster and an old yaller dog.

Chorus:
   Hoo-dle dang fol-di dye-do, hoo-dle dang fol-di day.
   Hoo-dle dang fol-di dye-do, hoo-dle dang fol-di day.

2. The Shanghai ran off and the cattle all died.
   The last piece of bacon that morning was fired.
   Poor Ike got discouraged and Betsy got mad,
   The dog wagged his tail and looked wondrously sad.

3. They soon reached the desert where Betsy gave out,
   And down in the sand she lay rolling about,
   While Ike in great terror, looked on in surprise,
   Saying, "Get up now, Betsy, you'll get sand in your eyes."

4. They crossed the wide rivers and climbed the high peaks,
   And camped on the prairie for weeks upon weeks.
   Starvation and cholera, hard work and slaughter,
   They reached California spite of hell and high water.

5. One morning they climbed up a very high hill,
   And with wonder looked down into old Placerville.
   Ike shouted and said, as he cast his eyes down,
   "Sweet Betsy, my darling, we've got to Hangtown."

6. Long Ike and sweet Betsy got married of course,
   But Ike, getting jealous, obtained a divorce,
   And Betsy, well satisfied, said with a shout,
   "Goodbye, you big lummox, I'm glad you backed out!"

The Ox Driving Song

Teams of oxen were used to haul freight to the growing settlements of the west. The men who drove these trains were called "bull whackers." It was their job to keep trade routes open, to supply forts and to bring wagon trains safely to their destination through any number of dangerous situations.

On the four-teen day of Oc - to - ber - o. I hitched my team in or - der - o to drive to the hills of Sa - lu - di - o. To me rol to me roll to me ri - de - o.

Chorus:
> To me roll, to me roll, to me ride-e-o,
> To me roll, to me roll, to me ride-e-o,
> To me ride-e-o, to me ride-e-ay.
> To me roll, to me roll, to me ride-e-o.

2. When I got there the hills were steep,
   T'would make a tender-hearted person weep,
   To hear me cuss and pop my whip,
   To see my oxen pull and slip.

3. I pop my whip and I bring the blood,
   I make my leaders take the mud,
   I grab the wheel, and I turn them around,
   One long, long pull and we're on high ground.

4. When I get home I'll have revenge,
   I'll land my family among my friends.
   I'll bid adieu to the whip and line,
   And drive no more in the wintertime.

Whoa! Ha! Buck!

This song has new words set to an older tune, in this case the well-known Turkey in the Straw. "Whoa Ha Buck" was heard often during the long trek west as drivers shouted commands to their oxen. Native Californians laughingly referred to the early settlers as "Wo-has." Travelers used buffalo chips (dried buffalo droppings) for fuel when there was no wood available.

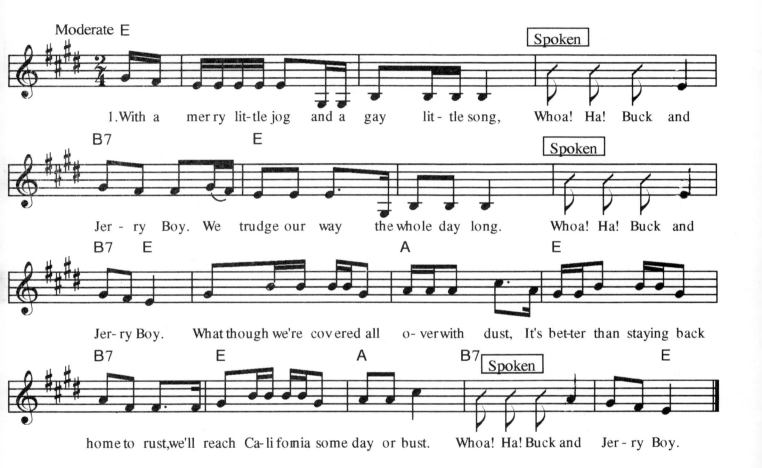

2. There's a pretty little girl in the outfit ahead,
   Whoa! Ha! Buck and Jerry boy,
   I wish she was by my side instead,
   Whoa! Ha! Buck and Jerry boy.
   Look at her now with a pout on her lips,
   As daintily with her finger tips,
   She picks for the fire some buffalo chips,
   Whoa! Ha! Buck and Jerry boy.

3. Oh, tonight we'll dance by the light of the moon,
   Whoa! Ha! Buck and Jerry boy,
   To the fiddler's best and only tune,
   Whoa! Ha! Buck and Jerry boy.
   Holding her hand and stealing a kiss,
   But never a step of the dance we miss,
   Never did know a love like this!
   Whoa! Ha! Buck and Jerry boy.

Out in the Wilderness

"Out in the Wilderness" could have been sung and danced by the light of the campfire after a long day's trek. It is a play-party (dance-game) in which players furnish their own music by singing.

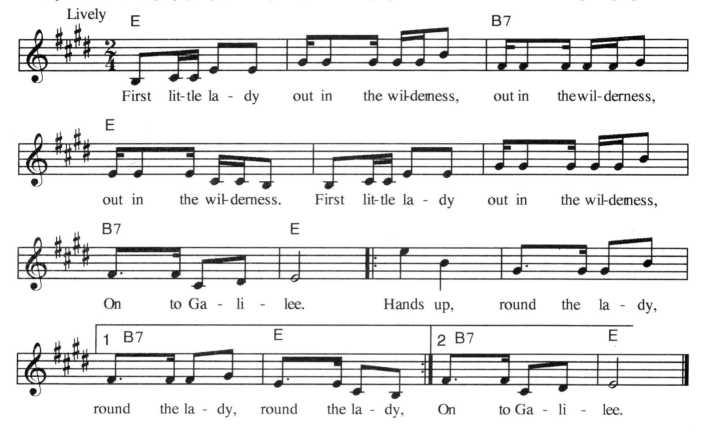

Lively

E ... B7
First lit-tle la - dy out in the wil-derness, out in the wil-derness,

E
out in the wil-derness. First lit-tle la - dy out in the wil-derness,

B7 ... E
On to Ga - li - lee. Hands up, round the la - dy,

1 B7 ... E
round the la - dy, round the la - dy, On

2 B7 ... E
to Ga - li - lee.

2. Swing that lady out of the wilderness etc.
Chorus
Hands up round the couple, round the couple, round the couple,
Hands up round the couple, on to Galilee.

Other calls include: "first old married lady," " first old hobo,"
"first old soapstick," ad lib others.

Dance instructions: Form circle, holding hands. Choose "first lady" by counting out
or otherwise.

First verse: All circle to right. "First lady" walks outside circle moving to left.
On the words "On to Galilee" she enters circle.

Chorus: Circle moves in four steps while raising hands and out four steps while lowering hands.
This action is repeated.

Second verse: Center dancer chooses a partner and they swing in the center while circle claps
and sings. Action for the chorus is the same except on words "on to Gallilee," the lady returns
to the circle and the new person walks around outside.

THE
GOLD RUSH
IN
SONG

PRINCIPAL MINING TOWNS OF THE CALIFORNIA GOLD RUSH

Sacramento River

Poker Flat

Downieville

Grass Valley • Nevada City

Auburn

Coloma

Placerville

Sacramento

Whiskey Flat

Angels Camp

Sonora • Columbia

Jamestown

• Mariposa

San Francisco

San Joaquin River

N
W • E
S

THE GOLD RUSH IN SONG

California was changed forever on that fateful day in January, 1848, when James Marshall discovered gold at John Sutter's mill. According to a local newspaper report in May, 1848, "The whole country from the seashore to the Sierra resounds with the sordid cry of 'Gold! Gold! Gold!' while the field is left half planted, the house is left half built and everything neglected but the manufacture of shovels and pickaxes."

By November, the New York papers were full of the news and the great surge to California began by land and sea. Although only six ships arrived in San Francisco Bay in 1848, by the end of 1849, more than 700 ships of every description had sailed in through the Golden Gate. Many were abandoned in San Francisco Harbor as seamen deserted to set out on foot for the gold country. They were soon joined by thousands more and Sierra sand bars, gulches and canyons rang with the sound of pickaxes and shovels.

The gold seekers were mostly young men between the ages of eighteen and thirty-five. They came from many different backgrounds and countries. Upon arrival they were transplanted into wild, unfamiliar surroundings and thrown together into rapidly formed communities beyond the reach of conventional customs. Fighting, thievery, hard drinking, and gambling were just a few of the problems to be encountered in this new, raw society.

Mining was a rough, monotonous job whose rewards seldom justified the sacrifice and labor devoted to it. In the first exciting days, the average miner made from ten to fifteen dollars a day and many made a hundred dollars or more Later, many miners, even working long, hard hours, could not make a living. Many realized that they could make more with less effort as merchants selling supplies to the miners.

Music and song played their part in mining life. With the availability of gold from free-spending miners, San Francisco and towns near the gold fields began drawing entertainers from all over the world. Wagon shows and makeshift circuses struggled up and down the steep mountain roads into isolated camps. Country fiddlers made as much as sixteen dollars a night performing in barrooms. Songs that told about the miners' lives and hardships began springing up. Many of these songs put new words to familiar melodies and took an amused, sometimes bawdy look at life at the gold camps. The songs were as rough and ready as the miners themselves and were sung lustily at saloons and around the campfires.

John Stone, a professional entertainer and former gold miner, who called himself Old Put, put together two collections of Gold Rush songs: "Put's Original California Songster" and "Put's Golden Songster." His songs caught the spirit and flavor of the Gold Rush and became very popular.

Oh, California!

This song, to the tune of Stephen Foster's "Oh, Susannah," became a rallying cry for those caught by the lure of gold. The gold seeker, with his washbowl (gold pan) on his knee, hoped to make a fortune.

I come from Sa-lem Ci-ty with my washbowl on my knee. I'm going to Ca-li-for-ni-ay the gold dust for to see. It rained all night the day I left, the wea-ther it was dry. The sun so hot I froze to death, oh bro-thers don't you cry. Oh Ca-li-fornia, that's the place for me. I'm bound for San Fran-cis-co with my washbowl on my knee.

2. I jumped aboard the 'Liza ship and traveled on the sea,
   And every time I thought of home, I wished it wasn't me!
   The vessel reared like any horse that had of oats a wealth;
   I found it wouldn't throw me so I thought I'd throw myself!

3. I thought of all the pleasant times, we've had together here,
   I thought I ought to cry a bit but couldn't find a tear.
   The pilot's bread was in my mouth, the gold dust in my eye,
   And though I'm going far away, dear brothers don't you cry.

4. I soon shall be in Fri-is-co and there I'll look around,
   And when I see the gold lumps there, I'll pick them off the ground,
   I'll scrape the mountains clean, my boys, I'll drain the rivers dry.
   A pocketful of rocks bring home, so brothers don't you cry!

98

The Lousy Miner

This is a song from Old Put's song collection. Like many Gold Rush songs, it is a catalogue of trials and hardships suffered for very little in return.

2. I've lived on swine till I grunt and squeal,
   No one can tell how my bowels feel,
   With flapjacks a-swimming 'round in grease,
   I'm a lousy miner, I'm a lousy miner,
   When will my troubles cease?

3. I was covered with lice coming on the boat,
   I threw away my fancy swallow-tailed coat,
   And now they crawl up and down my back,
   I'm a lousy miner, I'm a lousy miner,
   A pile is all I lack.

4. My sweetheart vowed she'd wait for me,
   Till I returned, but don't you see?
   She's married now, so I am told,
   Left her lousy miner, left her lousy miner
   In search of shining gold.

5. O land of gold, you did me deceive,
   And I intend you my bones to leave,
   So farewell home, now my friends grow cold,
   I'm a lousy miner, I'm a lousy miner
   In search of shining gold.

99

Joe Bowers

This is the tale of a traveler to California hailing from Pike County, Missouri. Perhaps Joe's brother was the same "Ike" who accompanied "Sweet Betsy" on her trek across the Western wilderness.

1. My name it is Joe Bow - ers, I've got a bro - ther Ike, I come from old Mis - sou - ri, yes, all the way from Pike; I'll tell you why I left there, and how I came to roam, And leave my poor old mam - my so far a - way from home.

2. I used to love a gal there, they called her Sally Black;
   I asked her for to marry, she answered me right back;
   Says she to me, "Joe Bowers, before we hitch for life,
   You ought to get a little home to keep your little wife."

3. O, Sally, dearest Sally, O, Sally for your sake,
   I'll go to California and try to make a stake,"
   Says she to me, "Joe Bowers, you are the man to win:
   Here's a kiss to bind the bargain," and she threw a dozen in.

4. At length I went to mining, put in my biggest licks;
   Went down upon the boulders just like a thousand bricks,
   I worked both late and early, in rain, and sun, and snow;
   I was working for my Sally, it was all the same to Joe.

5. At length I got a letter from my dear brother Ike;
   It came from Old Missouri, sent all the way from Pike;
   It brought to me the darndest news that ever you did hear,
   My heart is almost busting, so pray excuse this tear.

6. It said that Sal was fickle, her love for me had fled;
   She'd got married to a butcher, and the butcher's hair was red;
   And more than that, the letter said--it's enough to make me swear,
   That Sally had a baby, and the baby had red hair!

What Was Your Name in the States?

Once in the gold fields, the forty-niners were removed from social convention. A miner might never know or ask his partner's real name. "What Was Your Name in the States?" asks the question in a bemused way, assuming that the listener has come out West for a fresh start and a new identity.

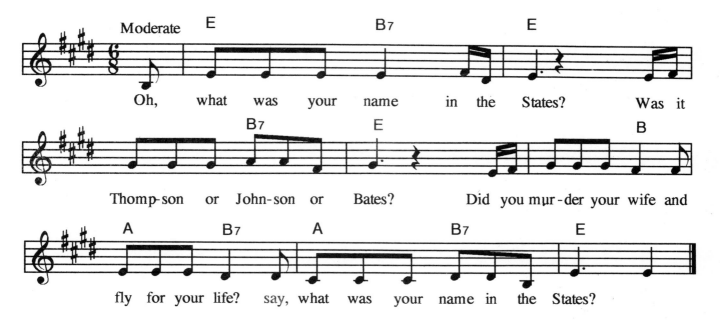

Oh, what was your name in the States? Was it
Thomp-son or John-son or Bates? Did you mur-der your wife and
fly for your life? say, what was your name in the States?

2. Did you leave your family at home? Did you come here anxious to roam?
   Did you find enough dust or did you go bust? Oh, what was your name in the states?

The Days of '49

In 1859, a Grass Valley minister observed, "The feverish excitement of the first mad years has now worn away. Gold-getting has assumed the form of a business and is no longer a game of chance." "Days of '49," remembers those rough and ready days when mining was still very much a "game of chance". Old Tom Moore is yet another hapless gold seeker whose efforts have come to nothing, yet he remembers fondly his old companions and the excitement of bygone days.

1. I'm old Tom Moore from the bum-mers' shore, In the good old gold - en days. They call me a bum - mer and a gin - sot, too, but what cares I for praise. I wan-der a-round from town to town, just like a rov-ing sign. And the peo-ple all say, "There goes Tom Moore of the days of for - ty - nine."

Chorus
In the days of old, in the days of gold, how of-times I re - pine, for the days of old when we dug up the gold, in the days of for - ty - nine.

The Days of '49

1. I'm old Tom Moore from the bummers' shore, in the good old golden days,
   They call me a bummer and a ginsot, too, but what cares I for praise.
    I wander around from town to town, just like a roving sign,
   And the people all say, "There goes Tom Moore of the days of forty-nine."

Chorus
   In the days of old, in the days of gold, how oftimes I repine,
   For the days of old when we dug up the gold, in the days of forty-nine.

2. My comrades, they all loved me well, a jolly saucy crew,
   A few hard cases I will admit, though they were brave and true;
   Whatever the pinch they ne'er would flinch, they never would fret or whine,
   Like good old bricks, they stood the kicks in the days of '49.

3. There was old Lame Jess, a hard old cuss, who never did repent;
   He never was known to miss a drink or ever spend a cent;
   But old Lame Jess, like all the rest, to death he did resign,
   And in his bloom went up the flume in the days of '49

4. There was New York Jake, the butcher's boy, he was always getting tight;
   And everytime that he'd get full he was spoiling for a fight;
   Then Jake rampaged against a knife in the hands of old Bob Sine,
   And over Jake they held a wake in the days of '49.

5. There was Ragshag Bill from Buffalo, I never will forget,
   He would roar all day and roar all night and I guess he's roaring yet;
   One night he fell in a prospector's hole in a roaring bad design;
   And in that hole, roared out his soul, in the days of '49.

6. Of all the comrades that I've had there's none that's left to boast,
   And I'm left alone in my misery like some poor wandering ghost;
   And as I pass from town to town they call me the rambling sign,
   There goes Tom Moore, a bummer, sure, of the days of '49.

Seeing the Elephant

"Seeing the elephant" was a popular Gold Rush expression. Thousands of forty-niners not only found little gold, but the hardships embittered them. Many felt they had been cheated, that the Gold Rush was a hoax. Like small boys at a circus, they had seen the elephant and had been disappointed.

1. When I left the States for gold, Ev-'ry-thing I had I sold. A stove a bed, a fat old sow, six-teen chick ens and a cow.

So leave you miners, leave, oh, leave you mi-ners, leave, Take my ad-vice, kill off your lice, or else go up in the moun - tains.

Chorus
Oh, no, lots of dust, I'm go-ing to the ci-ty to go on a "bust."

2. Being brave, I cut and carved, on the desert nearly starved,
   My old mule laid down and died, I had no blankets, took his hide.

3. The poor coyotes stole my meat, then I had nought but bread to eat;
   It was not long till that gave out, then how I cursed the Truckee route!

4. Because I would not pay my bill, they kicked me out of Downieville;
   I stole a mule and lost the trail, and then fetched up in Hangtown Jail.

5. When the elephant I'd seen, I'm darned if I thought I was green,
   And others say both night and morn, they saw him coming round the horn.

104

A Gust of Fall Wind

The Chinese were the largest foreign-born group to come to California during the Gold Rush (their numbers rose from 7 in 1848 to 20,000 in 1852). Lured by tales of *Gum Sahn*, the Golden Mountain, thousands left the overpopulated Kwangtung Province in southern China and were shipped to California by large placer-mining companies. In return for passage, the Chinese laborers agreed to work until they had paid off the debt with interest. Most expected to return ultimately to their homeland with new-found riches, but only a few realized this dream. This beautiful traditional song was sung by the Chinese in California and expresses the sadness of people exiled in a strange land and longing for home.

Tsa tsi chiu fung han. Bai Lu hu - a
A gust of fall wind blow-ing cold; A fall of white dew

chung shang. Ku shang nying pi - en ts' - ao.
turned to frost. The cruel frost freez - es each blade of grass, And the

Tsa man ts' - ao chao shang.
grass - hop - per dies in his gras - sy nest.

The text in Chinese characters:

乍 起 秋 風 寒　　酷 霜 凝 片 草

白 露 化 成 霜　　蚱 蜢 草 巢 殤

BIBLIOGRAPHY

Angulo, Jaime de, *INDIAN TALES*, Hill and Wang, New York, 1989.

Barrett, S.A. and Gifford, E.W., *MIWOK MATERIAL CULTURE, INDIAN LIFE OF THE YOSEMITE REGION*, Yosemite Natural History Association, Inc., Yosemite National Park, CA. 1933.

Black, Eleanora and Robertson, Sidney, *THE GOLD RUSH SONG BOOK,* The Colt Press, San Francisco, 1940.

Chevigny, Hector, *RUSSIAN AMERICA*, Binford and Mort, Portland, OR 1965.

THE CHINESE IN OAKLAND: UNSUNG BUILDERS, Oakland Chinese History Research, Oakland, CA, 1982.

Cleland, Robert G., *FROM WILDERNESS TO EMPIRE: A HISTORY OF CALIFORNIA*, 1542-1900, Alfred A. Knopf, New York, 1967.

Colcord, Joanna, *SONGS OF AMERICAN SAILORMEN,* W.W. Norton, New York, 1938.

Cummins, Marjorie, *THE TACHE-YOKUTS*, Pioneer Publishing Co., Fresno, CA, 1979.

Czarnowski, Lucille, *DANCES OF EARLY CALIFRONIA DAYS,* Pacific Books, Palo Alto, CA 1950.

Dana, Richard Henry, *TWO YEARS BEFORE THE MAST,* Penguin Inc., New York, 1964.

DaSilva, Owen Francis, *MISSION MUSIC OF CALIFORNIA,* Bancroft Library, University of California, Berkeley, CA.

Davidson, W., *WHERE CALIFORNIA BEGAN,* McIntyre, San Diego, CA.

Doerflinger, William, *SONGS OF THE SAILOR AND LUMBERMAN,* Meyer Books, Glenwood, IL 1972.

Dwyer, Richard A. and Lingenfelter, Richard E., *THE SONGS OF THE GOLD RUSH,* The University of California Press, Berkeley, CA, 1965.

Eargle, Dolon H., Jr., *THE EARTH IS OUR KEEPER, A GUIDE TO THE INDIANS OF CALIFORNIA, THEIR LOCALES AND HISTORIC SITES,* Trees Co. Press, San Francisco, CA 1986.

Emanuels, George, *CALIFORNIA INDIANS, AN ILLUSTRATED GUIDE,* Walnut Creek, CA 1990.

Fife, Austin E. and Alta S., *COWBOY AND WESTERN SONGS, A COMPREHENSIVE ANTHOLOGY,* Bramhall House, New York, 1982.

FORT ROSS: INDIANS, RUSSIANS, AMERICANS, Ft. Ross Interpretive Association, Jenner, CA 1980.

Godfrey, Elizabeth, *YOSEMITE INDIANS,* Yosemite Association, in cooperation with the National Park Service, 1977.

Hague, Eleanor, *EARLY SPANISH CALIFORNIA FOLKSONGS,* Bancroft Library, University of California, Berkeley, CA.

Hijar, Carlos, *RECUERDAS DE DON CARLOS N. HIJAR: CALIFORNIA EN 1834.* Dictated by author to Rosendo Corona for Bancroft Library, 1877, University of California, Berkeley, CA, 1877.

Hugill, Stan *SEA SHANTIES,* Barrie & Jenkins Ltd., London, 1977.

Hugill, Stan, *SHANTIES FROM THE SEVEN SEAS,* Routledge & Kegan Paul, London, 1984.

Jackson, Joseph Henry, *ANYBODY'S GOLD,* THE STORY OF CALIFORNIA'S MINING TOWNS, Chronicle Books, San Francisco, 1970.

Kirsch, Robert and Murphy, William, *WEST OF THE WEST,* E. P. Dutton, New York, 1967.

Lavender, David, *THE STORY OF CALIFORNIA,* California State Series, Sacramento, CA, 1971.

Lingenfelter, Richard E. and Dwyer, Richard A., *SONGS OF THE AMERICAN WEST,* University of California Press, Berkeley, 1968.

Locke, Eleanor G., *SAIL AWAY, 155 AMERICAN FOLK SONGS*, Boosey & Hawkes, 1988.

Lomax, Alan, *FOLK SONGS OF NORTH AMERICA*, Doubleday, 1960.

Lomax, John A., Lomax, Alan, Seeger, Charles, Seeger, Ruth, *FOLK SONG USA*, New York, Signet, Signet Classics, Mentor, Plum and Meridian Books, 1966.

Lummis, Charles, *SPANISH SONGS OF OLD CALIFORNIA*, G. Schirmer, Inc., 1923.

Morison, Samuel E. *EUROPEAN DISCOVERY OF AMERICA, Vol. II*, Oxford University Press, 1971.

Peatville, J., *MISSION MUSIC AND MUSICIANS*, Bancroft Library, University of California, Berkeley, CA.

Perez, Eulalia, *RECOLLECTIONS*, Bancroft Library, University of California, Berkeley, CA.

Powers, Stephen, *TRIBES OF CALIFORNIA*, University of California Press, Berkeley, CA, 1976

Ray, Sr. Mary Dominic, *GLORIA DEI*, Bancroft Library, University of California, Berkeley, CA.

SAN FRANCISCO SONGSTER, WPA Project, 1939-1942, Historical Songs of California, Research Project, Bancroft Library, University of California, Berkeley, CA.

Seidman, Laurence, *FOOLS OF '49*, Alfred A. Knopf, 1976.

Silber, Irwin and Robinson, Earl, *SONGS OF THE GREAT AMERICAN WEST*, New York, MacMillan Co. 1967.

Staniford, E., *THE PATTERN OF CALIFORNIA HISTORY*. Canfield Press, San Francisco, 1938.

Sunset Magazine Editors, *THE CALIFORNIA MISSIONS*, Lane Publishing Co., Menlo Park, CA.